UP CLOSE

SUBMARINES • FIGHTER PLANES
FIRE ENGINES • HEAVY EQUIPMENT

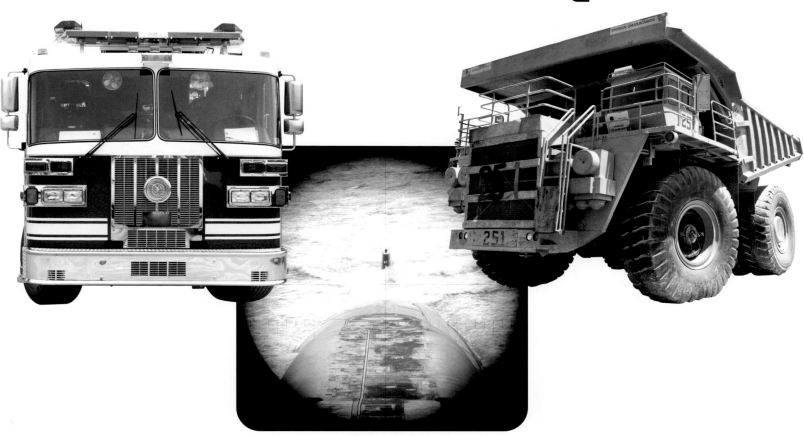

★ **Andra Serlin Abramson** ★

STERLING

New York / London
www.sterlingpublishing.com/kids

10 9 8 7 6 5 4 3 2 1

Published by Sterling Publishing Co., Inc.
387 Park Avenue South, New York, NY 10016
© 2007 by Sterling Publishing Co., Inc.
Distributed in Canada by Sterling Publishing
C/o Canadian Manda Group, 165 Dufferin Street
Toronto, Ontario, Canada M6K 3H6
Distributed in the United Kingdom by GMC Distribution Services
Castle Place, 166 High Street, Lewes, East Sussex, England BN7 1XU
Distributed in Australia by Capricorn Link (Australia) Pty. Ltd.
P.O. Box 704, Windsor, NSW 2756, Australia

Cover and interior design: Oxygen Design, Tilman Reitzle, Sherry Williams

Cover photo credits:
Front cover: (fighter plane) © Wernher Krutein / Photovault; (fire engine) © Robert Pernell / Shutterstock; (dump truck) © Benelux / zefa / CORBIS; (submarine) Gilbert King.

Back cover: (top: submarine) Gilbert King ; (center left: excavator) © Patrick Pleul / dpa / CORBIS; (center right: fighter plane) © Wernher Krutein / Photovault; (bottom right: firefighter) © Alan Schein Photography / CORBIS.

Front flap: (top right) © Tobias Bernhard / zefa / CORBIS; (center left) © Lester Lefkowitz / CORBIS; (center right) © George Hall / CORBIS; (bottom) © Wernher Krutein / Photovault; (background) © Glen Jones/Shutterstock.

Back flap: (first photo right) Gilbert King; (second photo center) © Aero Graphics, Inc. / CORBIS; (third photo center) © Wernher Krutein / Photovault; (fourth photo right) © Reuters / CORBIS; (background) © Aaron Kohr / iStockphoto.

Inside poster: © Wernher Krutein / Photovault.

Sterling ISBN-13: 978-1-4027-6012-9
        ISBN-10: 1-4027-6012-4

For information about custom editions, special sales, premium and corporate purchases, please contact Sterling Special Sales Department at 800-805-5489 or specialsales@sterlingpublishing.com.

CONTENTS

· · · · · · · · · · · · · · · ·

CONTENTS

FIRE ENGINES

HEAVY EQUIPMENT

UP CLOSE

INTRODUCTION

FIGHTER PLANES, SUBMARINES, FIRE ENGINES, AND heavy equipment can be found all around us—in the skies, beneath the seas, under our feet, and even on our streets. Whether today's tantalizing titanic technology protects, rescues, builds, harvests or recycles, it is awesome to behold.

Go behind the scenes and under the hood for a look at what it takes to put these sophisticated, gargantuan machines together. Learn how they operate, and discover some of their amazing components in actual size, including a fighter plane's cockpit and ejector seat button, a submarine's navigational computer display and periscope, a fire engine's cab and pump panel, and the hydraulic systems, gears, and bolts of colossal vehicles. All Up Close and at your fingertips.

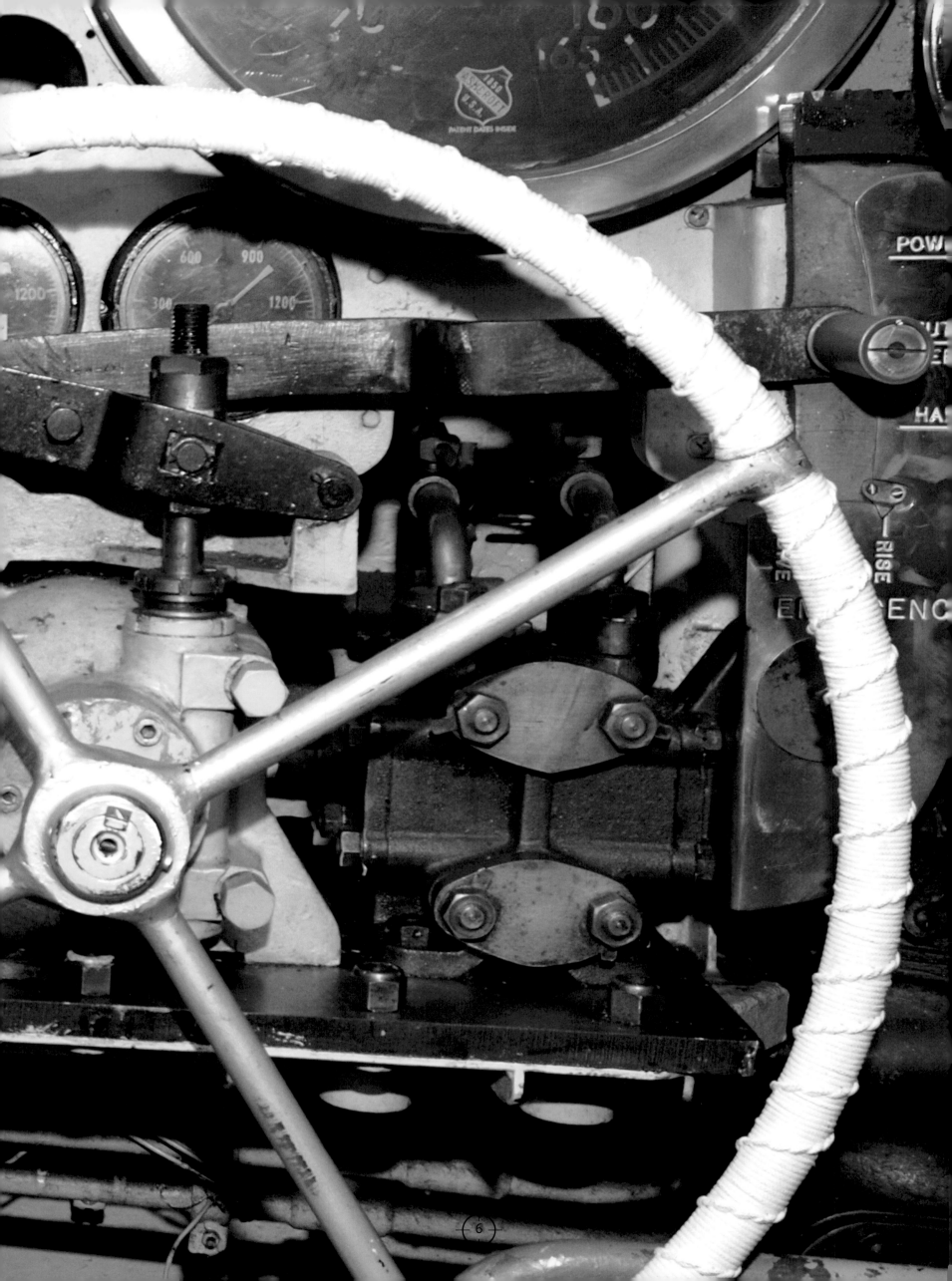

SUBMARINES

This Balao class submarine can support a crew of 10 officers and 65 men for a three-month patrol. It carries 24 torpedoes, each of which holds 600 pounds of "torpex," a high explosive.

AN UNDERWATER MARVEL

· ·

WITH NEARLY THREE-QUARTERS of the Earth covered by water, it is no wonder people have been dreaming of ways to travel under the oceans for centuries. As early as 1578, inventor William Bourne wrote of "a shippe or boate that may goe under the water to the bottom, and so come up again at our pleasure."

The USS Jimmy Carter—seen here moored under a protective magnetic "silencing" cape a naval base in Silverd Washington—is a nuclear-powered attack submarine the Sea Wolf class

By the American Revolution in 1775, an actual working submarine had become a reality. Submarines changed the way wars were fought, and in the nearly 250 years since the Revolutionary War, the American Navy has developed technology so advanced that most submarines are still considered "top secret."

Sailing on a submarine is a difficult but exciting career. More than 100 crewmembers live for months on a 300-foot-long, 30-foot-wide, three-story "building" with no windows.

There are two types of submarines. **Fast attack** submarines seek out and attack enemy ships using torpedoes and cruise missiles. **Fleet ballistic missile** subs carry long-range nuclear warheads.

Modern submarines can go anywhere in the world. This nuclear sub emerged from the ice at the Arctic Circle by using its strong metal top fin to punch a hole through the layers of ice.

HOW SUBS ARE BUILT

BUILDING A NAVAL SUBMARINE is a complex, time-consuming, and expensive proposition. Each ship can cost upwards of two billion dollars and may take several years to build. The pieces of the submarine are constructed in seven different shipyards around the country, the largest of which are in Newport News, Virginia, and Groton, Connecticut. The finished pieces are then transported to a central location to be put together.

It takes hundreds of workers with a wide range of skills—from heavy lifting to computer programming—to build a sub. Some researchers study the way fish swim to make submarines move more efficiently through the water. Other workers are responsible for welding the individual pieces of the submarine together. Still others are experts at hydraulics or engines. All these experts must work together to build one of the most technologically advanced machines ever created.

The hull, or outer shell, of the submarine is what keeps the crew safe from the surrounding water. The welded joints on the hull must be perfect.

Attack submarines are usually named after cities, such as the *USS Los Angeles*. Ballistic missile submarines are named after states, like the *USS Ohio*. The newest submarines, such as the *USS Jimmy Carter* (seen on page 8), are named for famous Americans and earlier classes of submarines.

Naval submarines are built from thousands of pieces in warehouses on dry land and are then carefully transported to the water.

DOWN THE HATCH

AIRTIGHT HATCHWAYS are the key to keeping the crew safe on a submarine. Submarines have exterior hatches that keep the water out and interior hatches that can be closed in case of an emergency. Knowing how to quickly and efficiently handle leaks is one of the most important skills a submarine crew can learn.

FIRE!

Aside from a leak, fire is another danger on a modern submarine. Most fires on a submarine are caused by faulty electrical components. Submarine crews are specially trained to put out fires, whether they occur in port or at sea. The crews carry out regular fire drills, but they do not wear fire boots or helmets. Instead, they wear special hoods called "SCBA"s, which stands for Self-Contained Breathing Apparatus. An SCBA is similar to civilian firefighting breathing devices.

The fire in the Commanding Officer's cabin on board this Canadian submarine caused a lot of damage but did not sink the sub.

Nuclear submarines have the added danger of the radioactive material they carry. The areas on the sub that carry the radioactive material are specially built to keep the crew safe. Subs also carry radiation suits for the crew to wear in case of an emergency.

The Navy has two rescue submarines that can navigate up to an injured submarine, attach to an escape hatch, and allow the crew to evacuate the sub.

ABANDON SHIP!

If an emergency forces the crew to abandon ship, they use an "escape trunk." The men put on special life preservers with hoods that provide the air needed to breathe. The hatch is then shut, and the trunk fills with water that is pressurized to sea pressure. Once this happens, the trunk's outside hatch opens, and the men are able to float to the surface.

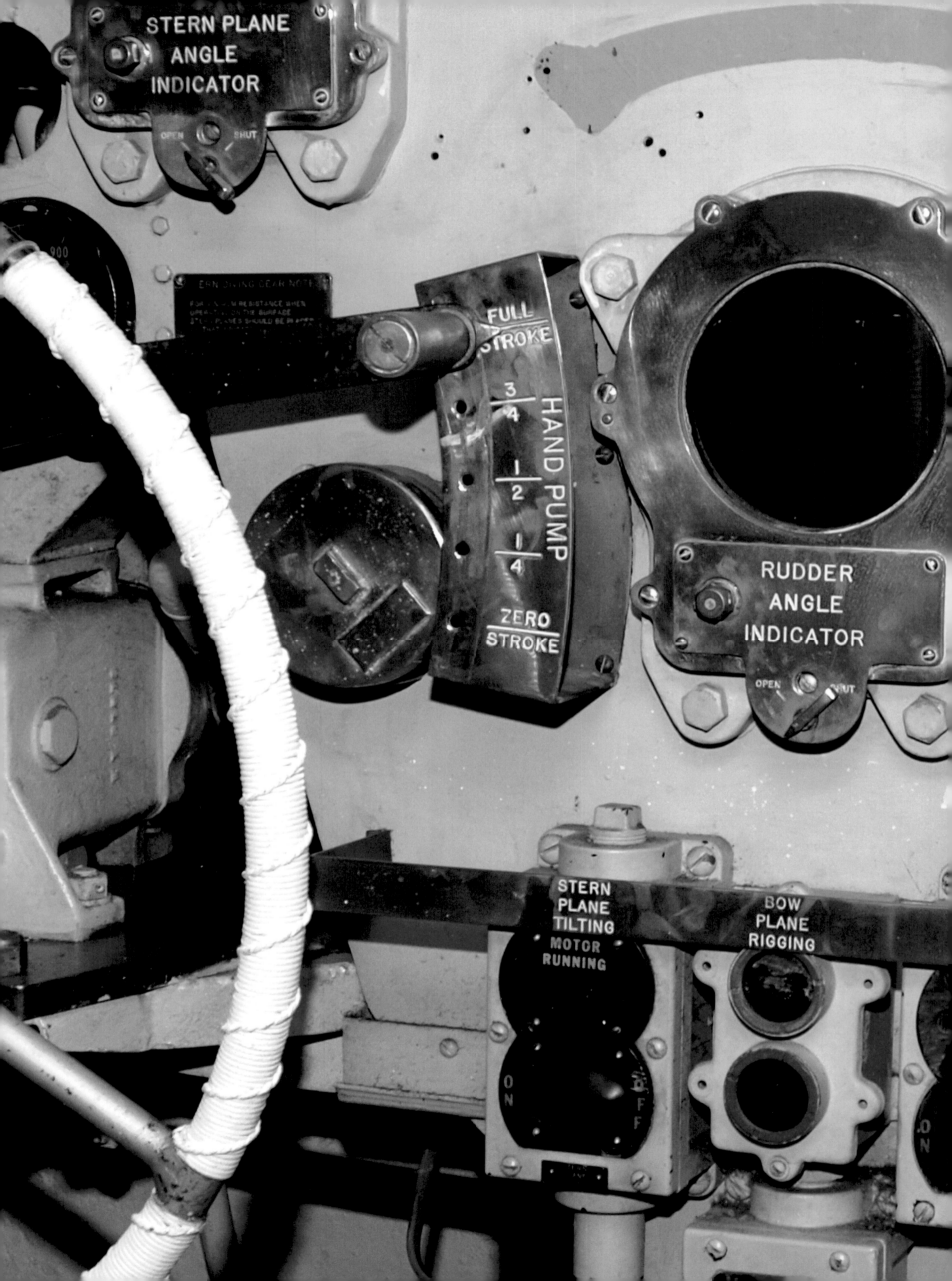

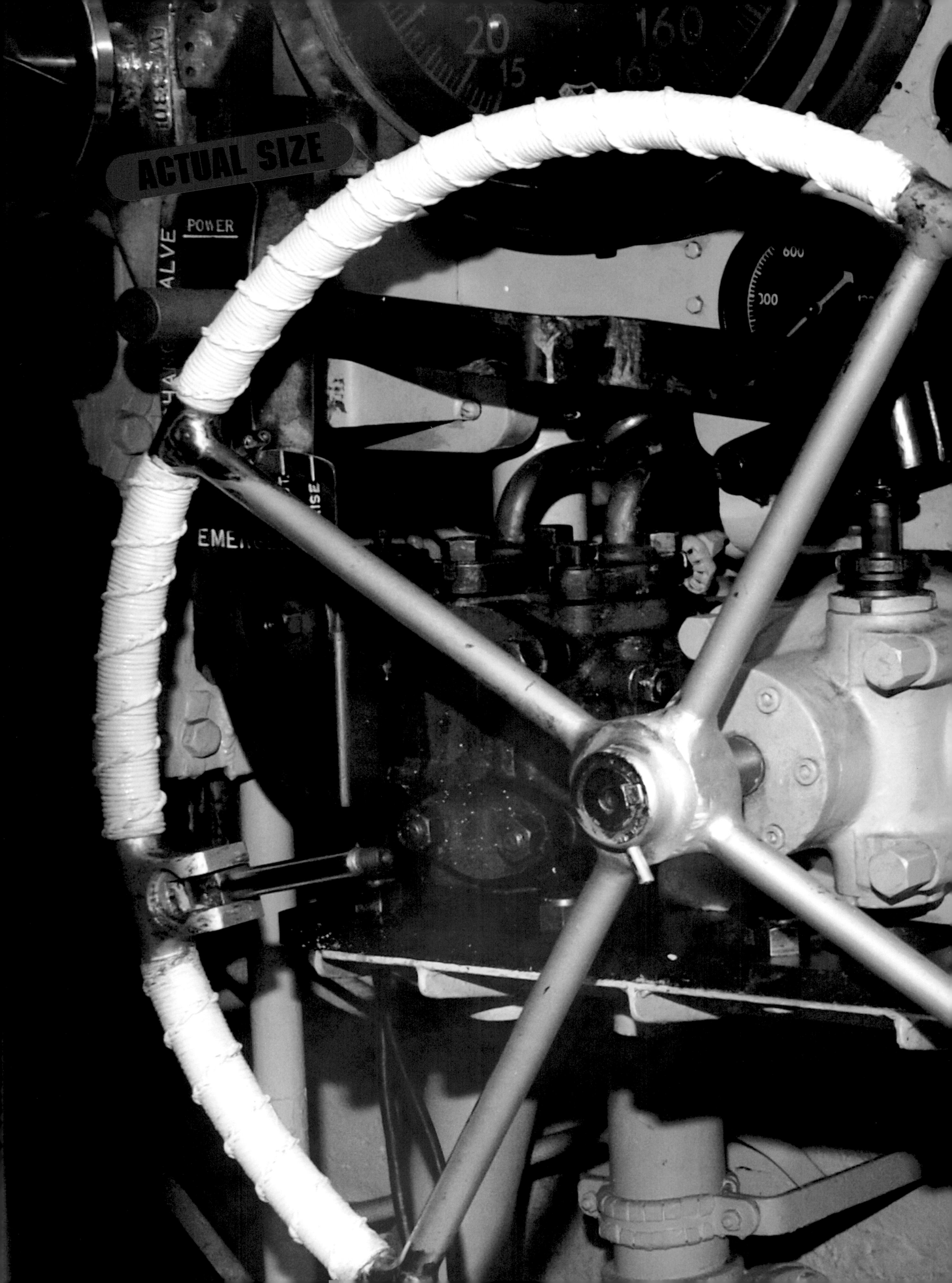
ACTUAL SIZE
POWER
20
160
15
600

STEERING THE SUB

SUBMARINES GO UP AND DOWN in the water by using ballast tanks situated throughout the submarine. Ballast tanks work by letting seawater in and out. To dive, the sub lets in more seawater. When the tanks contain less seawater, the submarine is lighter and rises to the surface.

There are two ways for a submarine to get to the surface once it is under the water. One way is for the sub to "blow" to the surface. This can happen at any depth by blowing high-pressure air into the ballast tanks. This causes the sub to become lighter and rise. The sub can also drive to the surface by changing the position of its "wings," which are found at the front and back of the sub.

Submarines are always painted black. The color helps them hide in the water. Keeping hidden is a principal task of a submarine.

ROCKING AND ROLLING

During normal weather conditions, a sailor on a submarine will feel much less rocking and rolling from the waves than a sailor on a boat at the surface of the water. It takes a large storm, such as a hurricane, to affect a submerged sub. Even in extremely violent weather conditions, the sub will roll only five to ten degrees. Compared to life on a surface ship, the ride is quieter and calmer.

Because the air on subs is continuously recycled and cleaned, submariners aren't used to outside smells. When the hatch is opened after months at sea, the smell of the ocean and other odors can seem very strong.

These sailors are at the helm of the USS Alabama, a Trident missile submarine.

INDICATOR
FULL STROKE
3/4
1/2
1/4
HAND PUMP
ZERO STROKE
BOW RIG. & WINDLASS CLUTCH
BOW RIGGING INDICATOR
300
1200

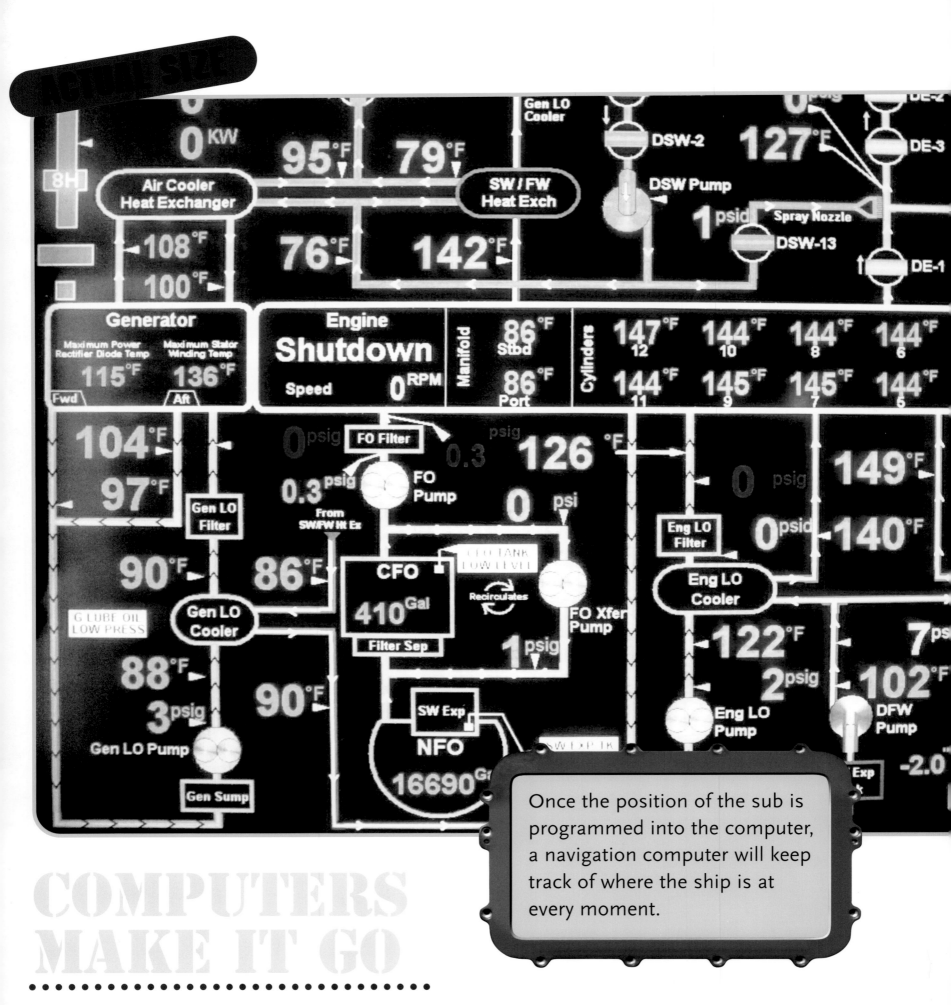

Once the position of the sub is programmed into the computer, a navigation computer will keep track of where the ship is at every moment.

COMPUTERS MAKE IT GO

SUBMARINES ARE SOME of the most technologically advanced machines ever created. Precision computers—such as the one seen above that monitors a diesel generator—assess every aspect of the submarine's environment. There are computers to check the status of the navigation system, atmosphere, sonar equipment, nuclear power, weapons, and all of the other systems.

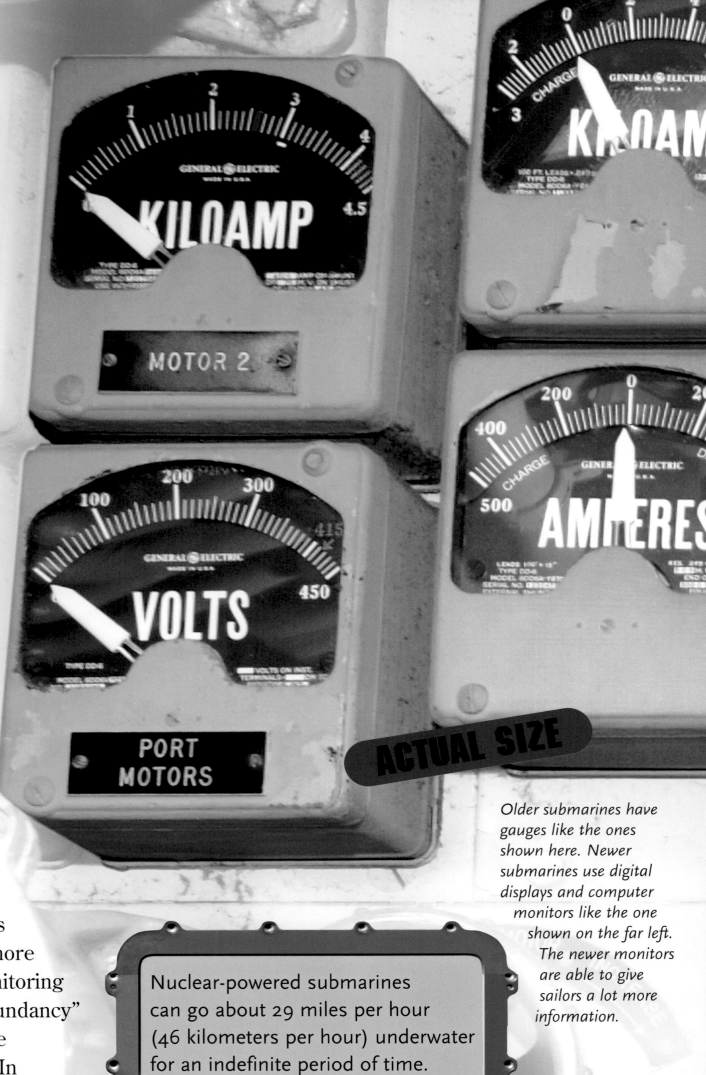

KILOAMP

MOTOR 2

VOLTS

PORT
MOTORS

ACTUAL SIZE

KILOAM

AMPERES

Older submarines have gauges like the ones shown here. Newer submarines use digital displays and computer monitors like the one shown on the far left. The newer monitors are able to give sailors a lot more information.

To ensure the safety of the submarine and its crew, subs often have more than one computer monitoring each system. This "redundancy" creates a backup in case anything breaks down. In addition, key systems such as hatches are routinely inspected and repaired by the crew.

Nuclear-powered submarines can go about 29 miles per hour (46 kilometers per hour) underwater for an indefinite period of time.

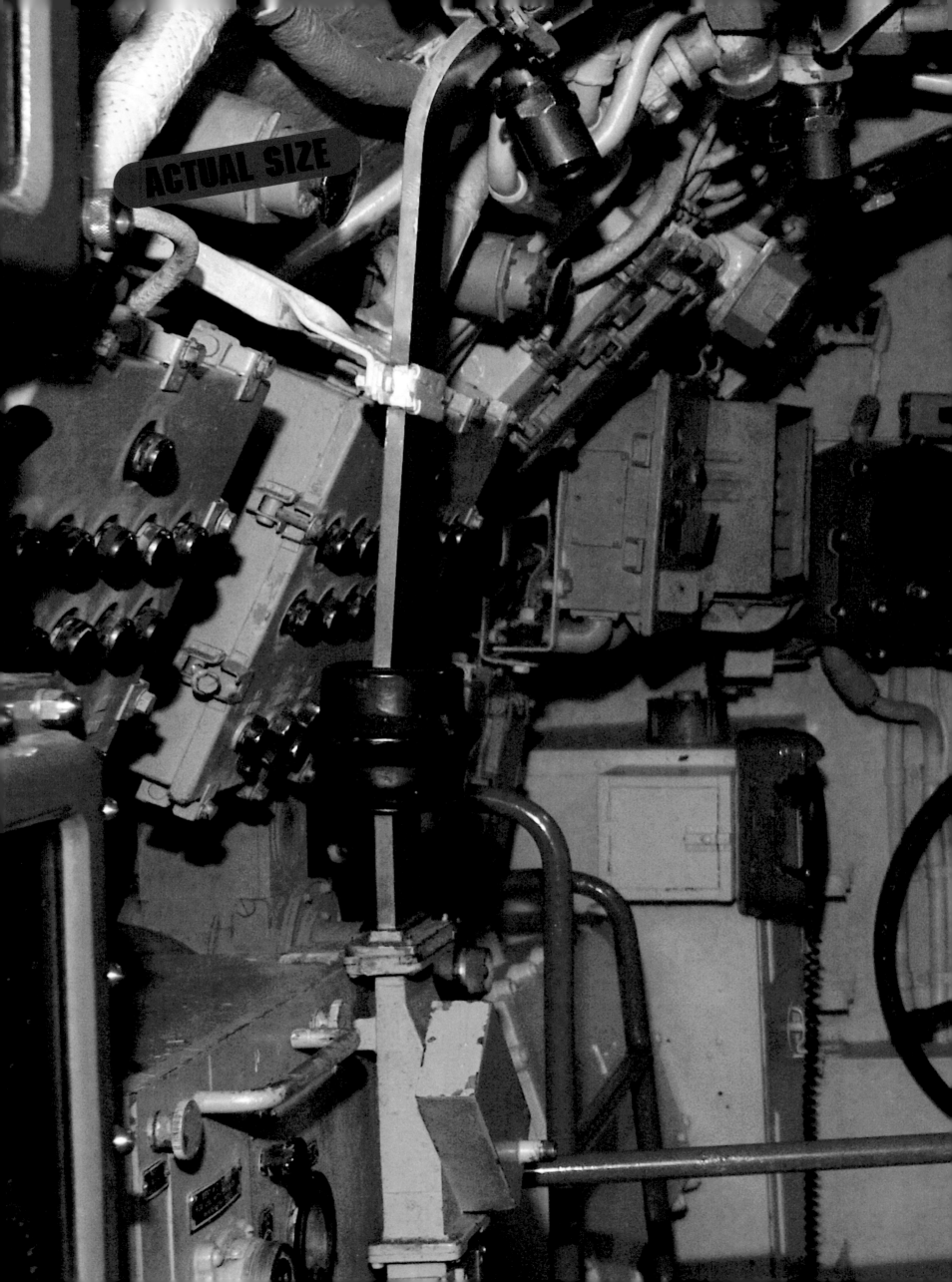

ACTUAL SIZE

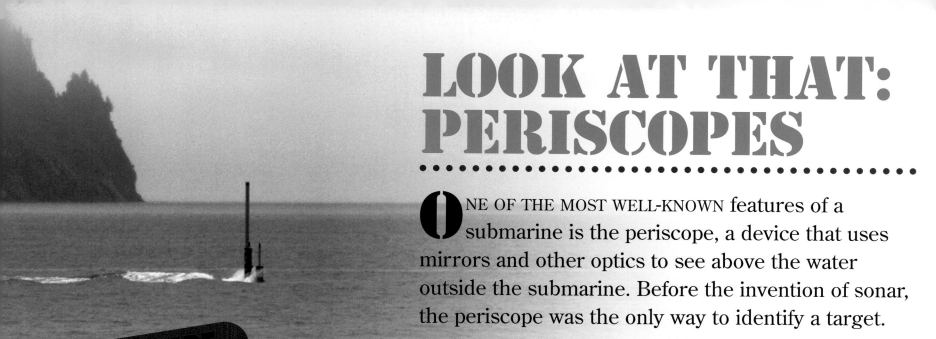

LOOK AT THAT: PERISCOPES

ONE OF THE MOST WELL-KNOWN features of a submarine is the periscope, a device that uses mirrors and other optics to see above the water outside the submarine. Before the invention of sonar, the periscope was the only way to identify a target.

A search periscope allows the submariner to look for both boats on the water and aircraft in the sky. Use of the periscope can be dangerous, though. Ships and planes can use the exposed periscope to locate the submarine under the water.

ACTUAL SIZE

A submarine needs three pieces of information to accurately attack a target: how far away it is (its "range"), the angle between the sub and its target (called the "aspect"), and the direction it is heading (known as its "bearing").

LOOK FOR YOURSELF

Looking through a real periscope is a lot like what you see in the movies. You'll see dashed lines on the eyepiece that help determine the range—the distance of a target from the sub. The periscopes on modern subs often have night vision cameras, internal antennas, and the ability to magnify the target.

SONAR: SOUND, NAVIGATION, AND RANGING

JUST AS WHALES use sound waves to find their prey, submarines use sonar to detect their targets. As a submarine cruises through the water, it creates noises that bounce off anything that is near it. A sonar computer evaluates these echoes and uses them to determine the location of the object.

ACTIVE OR PASSIVE?

Two different kinds of sonar are used to find enemy submarines and other targets. The first kind, passive sonar, just listens to the sounds around the submarine to see if anything is in the area. Passive sonar is most often used because it doesn't give away the sub's position. The second kind, active sonar, sends out a pulse of sound called a "ping." The time difference between when the ping is sent out and when the echo of the ping is heard bouncing off a nearby object helps the sonar operator measure the distance to the object.

Unfortunately, the ping can be easily detected by any submarine in the area, so using active sonar may allow the submarine to become a target instead of an attacker.

The sonar room on the USS Atlanta is lit with a blue light to make it easier for the sailors to read the monitors.

COMMUNICATION WITH THE OUTSIDE WORLD

Modern submarines use satellites to communicate with the outside world. Subs can send and receive voice and non-voice communication, and they can even get email. During long deployments at sea, the crew can also receive communication from home known as "family grams," a type of email that is sent through the Navy Information Operation Detachment (NIOD Groton).

During wartime, when a submarine needs to remain hidden, it may release a trailing antenna to receive news and intelligence from the outside world. A trailing antenna runs from the sub and floats on the surface of the water. It allows the sub to stay completely below water.

Sonar doesn't just pick up the sounds of other ships and subs. Sonar operators can hear whales, dolphins, and other sea creatures. They must be trained well to identify the many different sounds under the sea.

This conning tower is located directly above the submarine's control room.

SURFACE

BELL	AHEAD	
⅓	70 R.P.M.	70
⅔	140 R.P.M.	140
STD.	170 R.P.M.	
FULL	%	
EMERG.	100%	100

BATTERY

⅓	70 R.P.M.	70 R.P.M.
⅔	100 R.P.M.	100 R.P.M.
STD.	125 R.P.M.	125 R.P.M.
FULL	160 R.P.M.	160 R.P.M.
EMERG.	100%	100%

DECREASE

T. VM

THE CONTROL ROOM

• •

THE HEART OF THE SHIP is the control room. The Officer of the Deck stands his watch here, controlling all activities on board the submarine. In the control room, the ship's location is monitored, the course and depth are controlled, and all sonar contacts are tracked. The control room also functions as the attack center, where all of the ship's weapon systems are managed.

Crewmembers who drive the submarine are called the "helmsmen" and "planesmen." Their job is to keep the sub level. Like an airplane, the angle of the sub is adjusted by using a rudder and "wings" (called "diving planes") on the bow and stern. As seen in the photo below, sitting behind the helmsman and planesman is the diving officer who oversees them.

A TYPICAL DAY

Submarine crews are divided into three groups, or watch sections. Each group is on duty for 6 hours and then off duty for the next 12 hours, so a typical day on a submarine lasts 18 hours instead of the usual 24. During a regular day at sea, each watch will have about 25 crewmembers on duty at a time. However, when entering or leaving port, or when in battle conditions, every crewmember will have a watch station.

While on board a submarine, crewmembers wear a special uniform that's designed to be comfortable and reduce the amount of laundry each sailor creates. These one-piece coveralls are called "poopy suits."

During the 12 hours that a crewmember is not on watch, he can eat, sleep, attend training sessions, perform routine equipment maintenance, exercise, or just relax with a book, movie, or board game.

PROPULSION CONTROL 3W39A1
MADE FOR
BUREAU OF SHIPS
GENERAL ELECTRIC COMPANY
VOLTS 415 DRAWING LIST
U.S. PAT. 1822742
1875564 2027
SERIAL NO. 1945

CLUTCH HANDLE IN VERTICAL POSITION
FOR INDIVIDUAL TRIAL OPERATION

INCREASE VOLTAGE CREASE

INCR

GENERAL ELECTRIC

At the beginning of a long voyage, the amount of food required to feed the crew is far greater than the available storage space. Cans of food are stored on the floors of the sub throughout the ship.

MEALS UNDER THE SEA

IMAGINE BEING IN A windowless house for months at a time, never going outside or seeing the sun. That's what life is like for a submarine crew. It can be a long and difficult tour of duty with tight quarters and little access to entertainment. To keep morale high, the Navy makes sure the sailors on a submarine eat well. Each sub may have as many as four chefs who are trained much like the chefs on luxury cruise ships.

The amount of food a submarine takes on its voyage is the main limitation on how long the sub can stay at sea. Subs usually carry enough food for three months, plus a little extra for emergencies. Like all spaces on a sub, the galley—or kitchen—is cramped. Deep freezers, refrigerators, coffee makers, and other equipment take up most of the space. There is only a small work space for each member of the crew assigned to the galley.

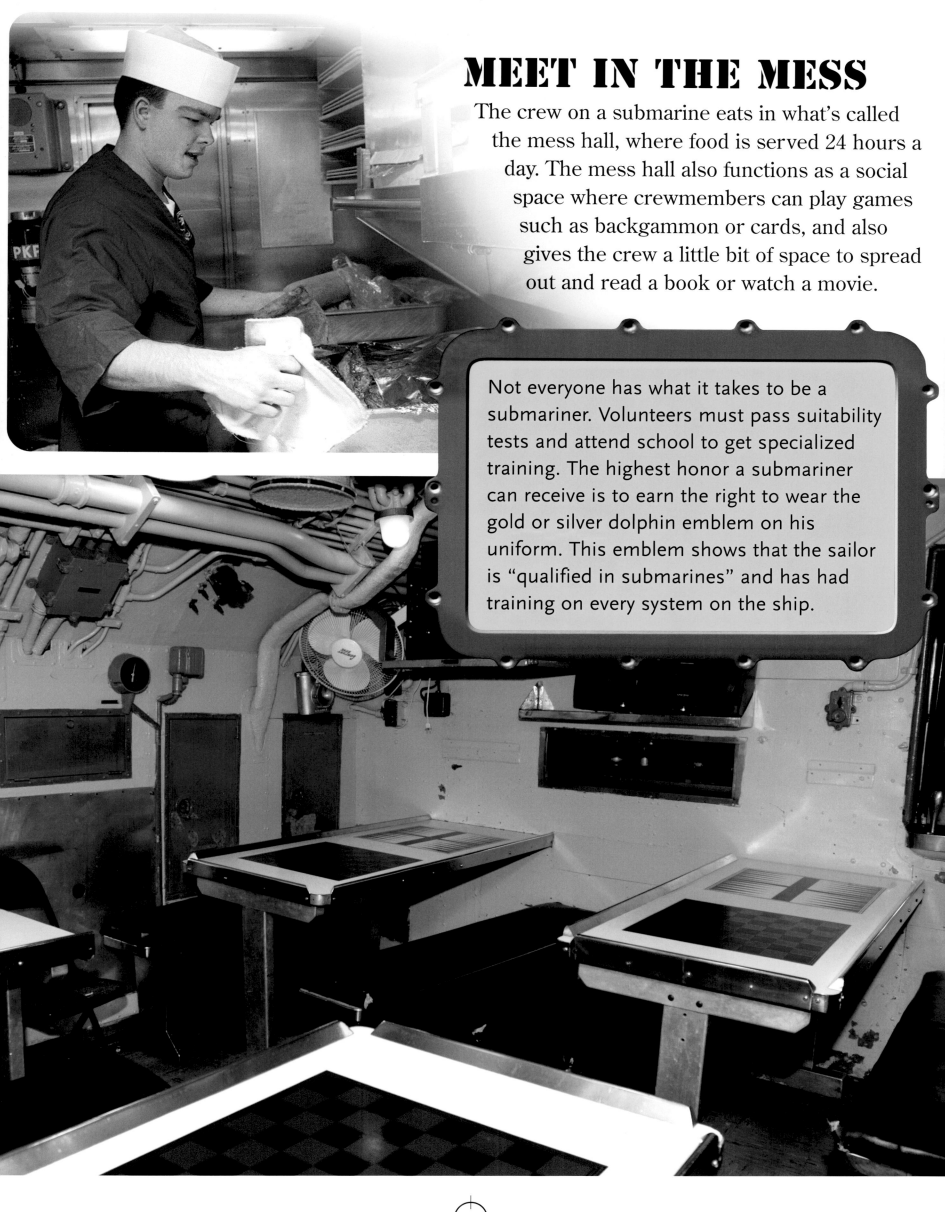

MEET IN THE MESS

The crew on a submarine eats in what's called the mess hall, where food is served 24 hours a day. The mess hall also functions as a social space where crewmembers can play games such as backgammon or cards, and also gives the crew a little bit of space to spread out and read a book or watch a movie.

Not everyone has what it takes to be a submariner. Volunteers must pass suitability tests and attend school to get specialized training. The highest honor a submariner can receive is to earn the right to wear the gold or silver dolphin emblem on his uniform. This emblem shows that the sailor is "qualified in submarines" and has had training on every system on the ship.

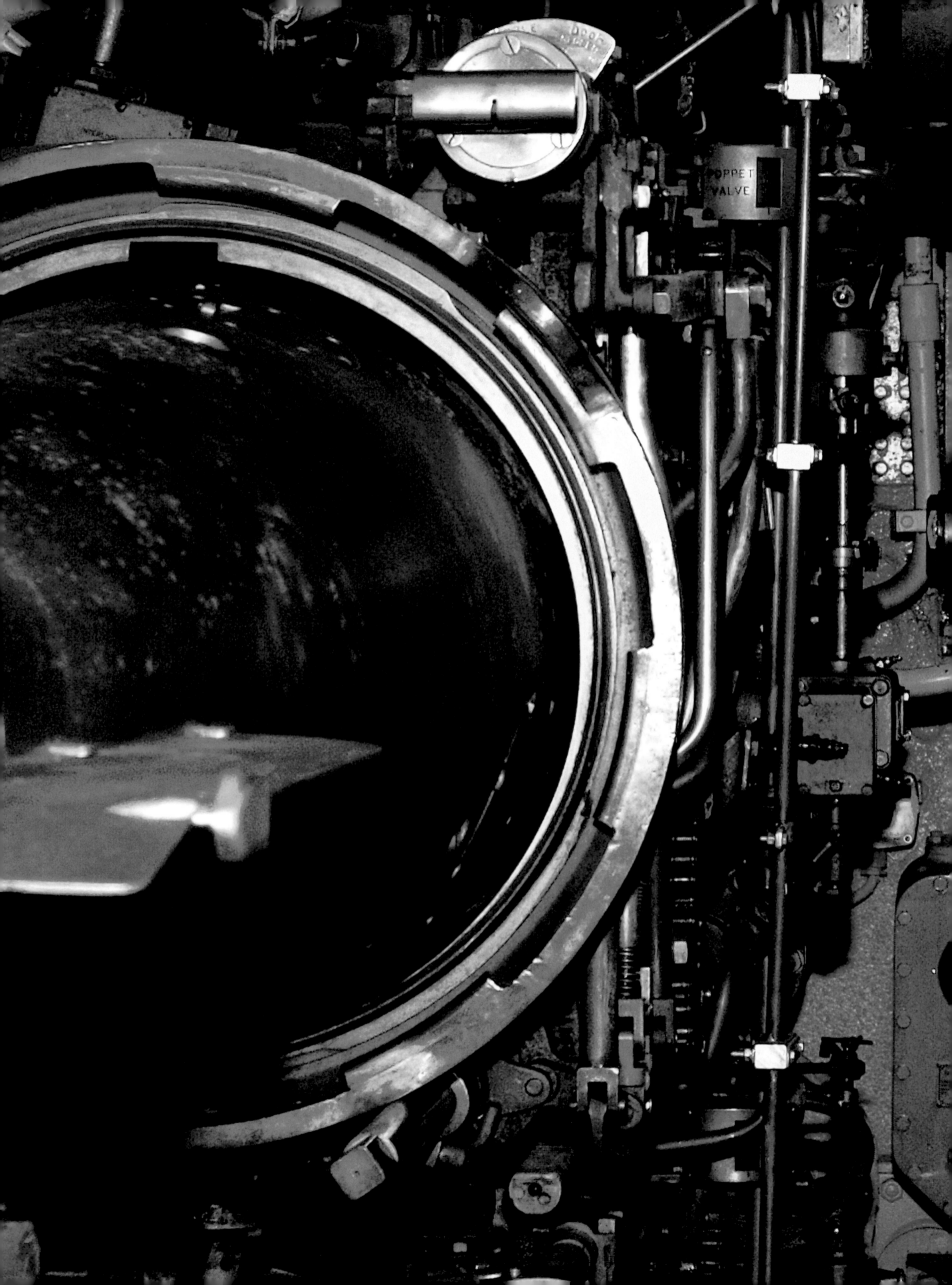

"MAN THE TORPEDOES!"

FOR A SAILOR ON A SUBMARINE, no words are more exciting or more dangerous. Torpedoes were first used on submarines during the 1870s, and by World War I, virtually every submarine carried this impressive weapon. The original torpedoes required the captain to correctly calculate the size, depth, and speed of the target in order to get a direct hit. Today's torpedoes use complex computer systems to guide the weapon where it needs to go.

To help protect the submarine in case of an attack, some subs have machine guns mounted on the deck.

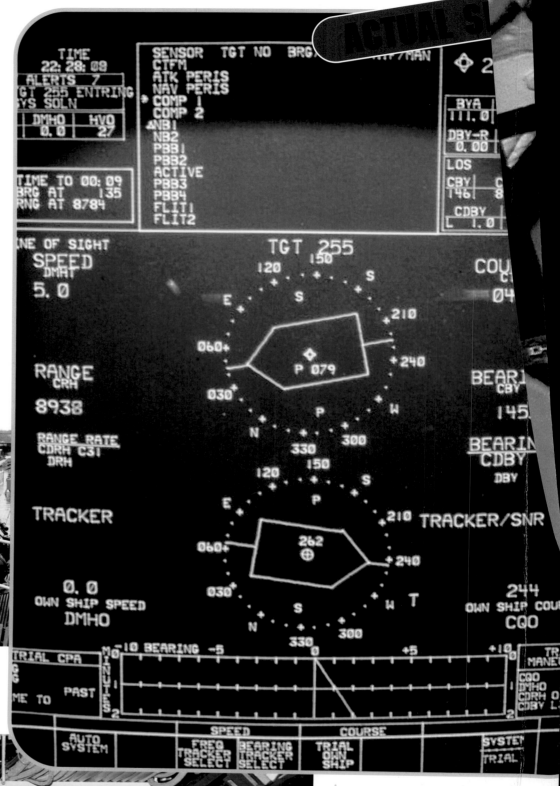

The screen above shows the torpedo fire control system on the Los Angeles class submarine USS Salt Lake City.

The open torpedo tube shown at left is on the USS Hartford, a Los Angeles class nuclear-powered fast attack submarine.

MODERN WARFARE

Modern-day submarines are equipped with missiles that can launch from underwater and attack targets thousands of miles away on land or at sea. Submarines may carry two different kinds of missiles. Ballistic missiles with nuclear warheads have thankfully never been used. They are deterrents that keep other nations from using nuclear weapons against the United States. Cruise missiles are capable of striking a specific spot hundreds of miles away.

Submarines may also carry torpedoes and mines. Mines can be laid without the submarine's location being given away. These mines are hidden in the water, usually in an enemy harbor or shipping lane, and can be programmed to go off only when they detect a ship nearby. Mines can even be programmed to allow a certain number of ships to pass by before the mine detonates.

A United States Navy fleet ballistic missile submarine carries as many as 24 Trident missiles with nuclear warheads. Each missile is stored in its own separate launch tube.

Everything on a submarine is constantly cleaned and monitored. Here, a sailor is cleaning a torpedo on the USS Norfolk.

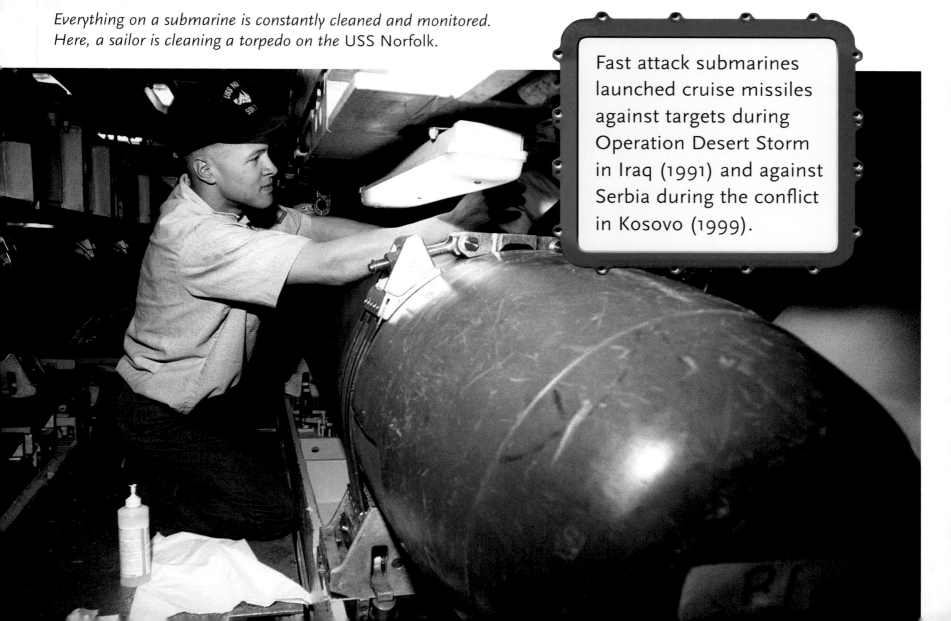

Fast attack submarines launched cruise missiles against targets during Operation Desert Storm in Iraq (1991) and against Serbia during the conflict in Kosovo (1999).

GOING TO THE HEAD

IN THE OLD DAYS, submarines carried a limited amount of fresh water and didn't have the power to recycle the water. As a result, sailors took very few showers. The one exception was the cook, who was allowed to take as many showers as he wanted in order to keep illnesses on board to a minimum.

On a submarine, fresh water is used for showers, sinks, cooking, and cleaning. Seawater is used to flush toilets, and the resulting "black water" is stored in a sanitary tank until it is pumped overboard using a special sanitary pump. Water from showers and sinks is stored separately in "gray water" tanks, which are pumped overboard using the drain pump.

WIPE DOWN SINK
AFTER EACH USE

Because there is so little room on a submarine, there is usually only one washer and one dryer on board. Laundry is done weekly by division on a rotating schedule.

Today, submarines are equipped with special machines that can remove the salt from seawater to keep the crew supplied with as much fresh water as they need, so shaving, showering, and even doing laundry is possible. Like on surface ships, the bathroom on a submarine is called the "head."

In order to keep working properly, submarines need regular maintenance. Usually a sub will head to a shipyard for the work it needs. Sometimes, though, they are serviced by floating ships called "tenders," as seen below. Tenders also have doctors and dentists aboard to address any health problems of the crew.

BERTHING AREAS

THE LIVING QUARTERS on a submarine are called "berthing areas." A berthing area has no more than 15 square feet of space for each crewman to sleep and store personal belongings. Each bunk on a modern submarine has a reading light, a ventilation duct, a curtain for privacy, and an earphone jack for the ship's on-board audio entertainment system.

The officers of the submarine share slightly more private quarters than the rest of the crew, with three people sharing one stateroom. Officers also have their own mess hall called the "wardroom."

Old-time submarines often had so little usable space that sailors slept side-by-side with the torpedoes. As you can see in the photo above, some bunks were even suspended just above weapons.

Women are not currently allowed to serve as submariners in the U.S. Navy. This is because of the limited amount of privacy and the lack of space for separate sleeping and bathroom areas.

Even modern submarines allow each sailor very little personal space.

FIGHTER PLANES

Pilots say that flying a high-tech fighter plane is a thrill that comes with great responsibility. Fighter planes provide air support to all branches of the military.

LYING HIGH

IGH-TECH FIGHTER PLANES are at the forefront of our country's defense. Able to scramble into action in utes, capable of reaching speeds of Mach 3 (three s the speed of sound), and able to drop bombs, oy missiles, and perform amazing acrobatic feats, er jets have captured our imaginations and made ions of people dream of streaking through the sky.

UILDING A FIGHTER JET

eral important issues must be kept in mind en designing a fighter plane. First, the ght and size of the plane must be sidered. If the plane is too heavy, ill not be able to take off from short runway of an aircraft rier. If it is too big, it will not agile enough to avoid smaller my planes.

Designers must also think of w far the plane will need to el (its range) and how fast it need to go.

The Germans were the first to use jet-powered planes in combat. The Messerschmitt Me 262, which they used during World War II, could fly almost 550 miles per hour (885 kilometers per hour)—faster than any other plane at the time.

Employees at Lockheed Martin's F-22 Raptor production facility attach a tail fin to the body of Raptor AK087.

Finally, the designer must keep in mind the cost of producing the plane. If the plane is too expensive, even rich countries like the United States may not want to buy it.

Because of the huge expense involved in designing and manufacturing a fighter plane, several companies often work together to create different pieces of the same jet.

AIRCRAFT CARRIERS

THE LARGEST WARSHIPS on the ocean are aircraft carriers. These floating air bases are capable of carrying more than 80 planes. The longest aircraft carrier is the *USS Enterprise* (CVN-65), which is 1,123 feet (342.3 meters) long. The letters "CVN" indicate the type of ship. The classification "CV" is for aircraft carriers. The "N" means it is nuclear-powered. The number after the "CVN" is the number of the aircraft carrier.

Although aircraft carriers carry a variety of built-in weapons, their large size and relatively slow speed make them vulnerable to attack, so they often travel in battle groups. A battle group may contain attack submarines, cruisers, destroyers, and other support ships. Aircraft carriers are also protected by the fighter planes they service.

The steam you see rising from the deck of the aircraft carrier USS Enterprise *(CVN-65) is caused by a steam catapult that is used to launch fighter jets into the air.*

The *USS George H. W. Bush* (CVN-77) will be the tenth and final aircraft carrier of the Nimitz class when it begins service in 2008. A new class of ships will be launched in 2015.

An experienced flight crew on an aircraft carrier can launch or land a plane every 25 seconds.

FIGHTER PLANE ENGINES

BEFORE JET ENGINES were developed in the 1930s, planes used propellers and piston engines (similar to car or motorcycle engines) to thrust the plane forward. Planes flying with a propeller could achieve speeds of around 400 miles per hour, but only by burning a lot of gas, making long, nonstop flights impossible. The development of the jet engine helped the military create planes that could fly more than three times the speed of sound (770 mph/1,239 kph).

The cracking sound made by a bullwhip is actually a sonic boom. The end of the whip, called a "cracker," moves faster than the speed of sound.

AFTERBURNERS

Military jets use afterburners—an extended exhaust system containing extra fuel injectors—to get more speed from the plane. The big advantage of afterburners is that they significantly increase the thrust of the engine without adding much weight or complexity to it. The disadvantage of afterburners is that they use a lot of fuel to generate power. As a result, most planes use afterburners sparingly.

SONIC BOOM

As a plane travels through the air, it forces the air that it encounters to move out of the way in the form of waves. As the plane approaches the speed of sound, the waves cannot get out of the way fast enough, and the plane comes up against what's called the "sound barrier." The boom that people on the ground hear when a plane crosses the sound barrier is called a "sonic boom."

You can actually see what happens to the air as this plane reaches the speed of sound.

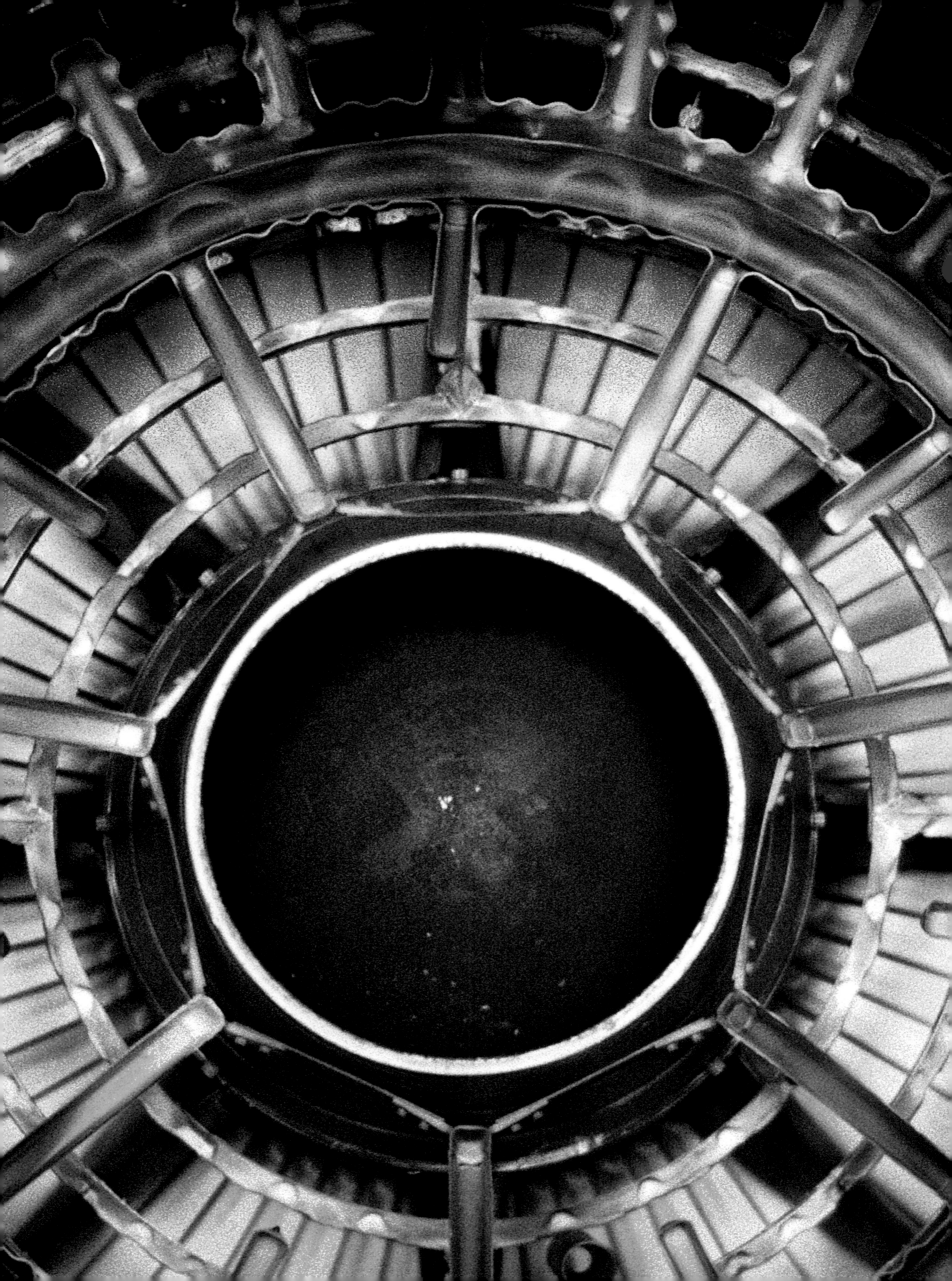

THICK-SKINNED

· ·

THE OUTER HULL, OR SKIN, OF A FIGHTER JET needs to be able to withstand extreme temperatures of both hot and cold. The air temperature at high elevations is very cold. Extreme heat results from the intense friction caused by the rush of air over the plane at high speeds.

Today's fighter planes are made of composite materials. The term "composite" means that different materials are used together to keep the weight down, or provide strength or other benefits. In many planes, including the advanced F-22, titanium is the most-used material because of its heat-resistance qualities and its high strength-to-weight ratio. Other materials used include aluminum and thermoplastic.

DANGER

EJEC
SE

DANGER

ACTUAL SIZE

EJECTION SEATS

In the event of an emergency, the pilot's last resort is to hit the ejection button and evacuate the plane. In most cases, the ejection seat is powered by a rocket engine that propels the seat, with the pilot in it, out of the plane. The seat then releases a parachute that carries the pilot to safety. Attached to the ejection seat are a raft and other supplies to help the pilot survive until help can arrive.

The ejection button is used by pilots when there are no other options. Besides being responsible for losing a plane worth millions and millions of dollars, pilots know that being shot out of a jet can be dangerous and painful. However, with thousands of lives saved, ejection seats will continue to be used by fighter plane pilots.

Live testing of ejection systems over the years has included humans, chimpanzees, and even bears.

ACTUAL SIZE

EMER STORES
JETTISON

BRAKES
CHAN 1

PARKING
BRAKE

CHAN 2

ANTI-

Hitting the ejector seat button is not a decision a pilot makes lightly. Being propelled out of a fast-moving fighter plane is a dangerous and scary exercise.

A laser-guided missile creates a heat signature for a specific target. After the missile is launched, it uses its onboard instrumentation to locate the heat signature. The missile is able to find the target even if the target is moving.

With only a limited number of missiles per plane, pilots know that they need to use them wisely.

WEAPONS

A IRPLANES WERE FIRST USED for military purposes during World War I. These first planes were not fighters, but rather spies. Their job was to make passes over enemy territory and report the enemy's movements back to their commanders.

Originally, these spy planes did not carry weapons. If two enemy planes passed each other in the sky, the pilots would wave and continue on their way.

Eventually, planes were fitted with machine guns, and modern fighter planes were born. Today's fighter planes have multiple weapon capabilities, including guns, missiles, and bombs. They can attack both enemy planes in the air and targets on the ground.

At Bagram Air Base in Afghanistan, a Tech. Sgt. with the Aircraft Maintenance Squadron inspects a Gatlin gun on an A-10 Thunderbolt. Air Force planes are carefully inspected every 400 flying hours.

This TV/IR smart bomb features a video camera that allows the pilot to locate and lock onto a target.

ACTUAL SIZE

THE RED BARON

The most famous fighter pilot of all time was a German named Manfred von Richthofen, known as the Red Baron. During World War I, the Red Baron shot down more than 80 enemy planes. In 1918, the Red Baron was defeated in battle over the fields of France by a Canadian pilot named Captain Roy Brown. Captain Brown used the position of the sun to blind the Red Baron and managed to get the upper hand, sending the world's most famous fighter pilot to his death.

Developed in 1947, the radar-guided, subsonic Firebird missile was the first U.S. guided air-to-air missile. It became obsolete within a few years with the development of supersonic missiles such as the AIM-4 (AIM stands for air-intercept missile) Falcon, the AIM-9 Sidewinder, and the AIM-7 Sparrow.

Missiles are heavy and must be handled with care.

TAKEOFFS AND LANDINGS

. . . .

APLANE'S LANDING GEAR must be able to support the full weight of the plane as it lands at more than 100 miles per hour and comes safely to a stop. Today's planes use three strategically positioned wheels to spread the weight over as large an area as possible. (The wheels retract into the plane's hull to cut down on air resistance during flight.) Some planes need assistance to land safely. The F-4 Phantom shown in the picture above uses a parachute-type of device to help it slow down after landing.

Just like on an automobile, the tires on the landing gear of airplanes must be carefully inspected and replaced whenever wear is found.

TAKING OFF FROM AN AIRCRAFT CARRIER

One of the trickiest maneuvers a pilot can perform is to take off from or land on an aircraft carrier. Because the carrier is not entirely still in the water and has a much shorter runway than an airport, a pilot must aim for a moving target and adjust the speed and altitude of the plane very precisely in order to achieve a safe takeoff or landing.

Most fighter planes take off from an aircraft carrier by using a catapult. The planes have hooks that are attached to runners along tracks on the deck of the ship. A spring, explosive charge, or even steam is used to propel the runners forward at a great speed, launching the plane into the air.

Modern aircraft carriers have angled flight decks. The angled deck landing area is to allow aircraft that miss the arresting wires (called "bolters") to gain altitude again without hitting aircraft parked on the forward parts of the deck. The angled deck also allows some aircraft to take off at the same time as others land.

Here's a photo of the landing gear on a North American P-51 Mustang fighter, used in World War II.

AN "ARRESTING" MOMENT

A fighter plane lands on an aircraft carrier by lowering a hook from its tail that catches an "arrester wire" stretched across the flight deck. Tailhook aircraft rely on a landing signal officer (LSO) to control a plane's landing approach. The LSO checks the altitude, attitude (the orientation of the plane relative to the carrier), and speed of an approaching plane and transmits that data to the pilot.

3

NO STEP

WINGS

· · · · · · · · · · · · · · · · ·

THE WINGS ON DIFFERENT PLANES have distinct and important differences that affect how each plane is able to take off, land, and maneuver in the air.

The look of the wings is an important consideration in the design of a plane. Designers must think about the flaps, slats, and the angle of attack (the angle that the wing presents to oncoming air).

The flaps are used during takeoff and landing. They are extended rearward and

The shape of the wings of the F-117A Stealth Bomber helps make the plane invisible to radar.

downward from the trailing edge of the wings, allowing the wing to turn more air and thus create more lift. Slats, like flaps, temporarily alter the shape of the wing to increase lift, but they are attached to the front of the wing instead of the rear.

With the horizontal tail wing, the pilot can change the plane's angle of attack, and therefore control whether the plane goes up or down. With the vertical tail wing, the pilot can turn the plane left or right.

The part of the plane that actually initiates a turn is called an aileron, French for "little wing." The two ailerons are located on the tip of each wing and can go up and down at opposite times, producing a rolling movement.

THE CONTROL STICK

PILOTS USE A CONTROL STICK (or joystick) to adjust the movement of a plane. Unlike a car, which can only be steered to the left or the right, an airplane can go left, right, up, or down. To keep the plane level and on course, a pilot must have good coordination and be well-skilled at using his or her control stick.

To climb, a pilot pulls back on the control stick, which raises the nose of the plane. The wings of the plane are now at a greater angle to the wind, which will give the plane more lift if there is enough power in the engines. To dive, the pilot pushes the control stick forward, pitching the nose downward.

Agile fighter planes can easily do maneuvers such as rolls, vertical climbs, and steep drops. A pilot may experience weightlessness during some maneuvers and, in others, be subjected to extreme g-forces (acceleration due to gravity) that make him or her practically unable to move. Fighter plane control sticks are designed to respond to a pilot's command, even if he or she can barely move. Just the twitch of a finger can bring the plane out of a dive or launch a weapon.

THE LITTLE BLACK BOX

All fighter planes (and commercial airlines) carry a flight data recorder, also known as a black box. The box—which is actually almost always red so it can be easily located in case of a crash—is a recorder that is connected to every major system of the aircraft and that keeps record of everything that happens during a flight, including the performance of every instrument. The box is housed in a titanium case that is designed to protect it in case of a fire or crash.

A second black box is called the cockpit voice recorder, which records all the sounds in the cockpit of the plane, including engine noises, the pilot's voice, and radio transmissions.

THE INNOVATIVE F-16

The first plane that used an innovative design feature called a "fly-by-wire" control system was the F-16. Before this innovation, the pilot would move a control stick connected to the plane's wings, ailerons, and rudder. In the F-16, a computer moves the control surfaces in response to electronic input from the pilot's control stick. The fly-by-wire computer automatically makes split-second corrections to keep the plane stable.

DECM
ON
OFF
TEST
KNOTS
TEST
CLI—M
DI—VE
BUNO 15699
ALT
1000 FT
100 FT
IN. HG
3004
MILES
HOOK
LIFT
UHF NORM
FUEL QUANTITY
LBS X 1000
LBS X 1000
ACCELERATION
G UNITS
FIRE

ACTUAL SIZE
EMER
STORES
JETTISON
ANGLE OF ATTACK
30
0
10
RADAR
ALTITUDE
400 600
200
1000
150
2000
100
3000
50
0
5000
LANDING
HARNESS
ARMAMENT
FLAPERON
HOOK
WHEELS
FLAPS
FUEL
AUTO PILOT
SWITCH DIMMERS
PANEL
RADAR
DESIGNATOR
GRAPHICS
STATUS
%RPM
EGT
VERTICAL
DISPLAY
BRT
CONTRAST
PITCH TRIM

HE COCKPIT

STRUMENTATION IN THE COCKPITS OF
modern planes is impressive, with
mputers monitoring everything from
use to weather conditions, airspeed
rojected course, weapon readiness
ossible targets. Information is
played on monitors, like the one on
right, or sometimes even projected
the windshield of the cockpit to
w the pilot to keep his or her eyes
the sky at all times.

IGH-TECH
O THE MAX

e cockpit of the F/A-22 fighter
ne has a heads-up display (HUD)
t projects information in front of
e pilot's view, showing target status, weapon
tus, and cues that indicate if the
eapons are locked on the target.
e primary display provides a view
the air and ground tactical
uation. Two smaller displays

show communication,
navigation, and flight
information. Three
secondary displays
show air-threat and
ground-threat data.
The goal is to make
it simple for the pilot
to process all the
information that is
displayed.

ghter plane cockpits have
ge windows that allow
ots to see in all directions.

ACTUAL SIZE

DETECTION ANGING

...h stands for Radio Detection ...ng, uses radio waves to locate ...nes, ships, or other objects. ...rks by sending an electrical ...o the air. The signal, called a ...ve, bounces off nearby objects, ...echo can be detected by the ...giving the location of the object.

...he top secret Stealth Fighter is ...lmost invisible to radar! The ...materials it is constructed from absorb radio waves so the waves never return to the sender. Also, the plane's shape causes radar beams to scatter so the location of the plane can't be detected.

The artificial horizon shown above is an instrument used to show the pilot where the plane is in relation to the ground.

PILOTS AND FLIGHT OFFICERS

FIGHTER PILOTS MUST be ready to go at any moment, able to defend their ship, base, or country from an attack. Pilots in the military are trained in air-to-air combat, bombing, search and rescue, aircraft carrier takeoffs and landings, over-water navigation, and low-level flying.

Student aviators learn about aerodynamics, aircraft engineering, navigation, and meteorology. They must be in top physical condition to withstand the stress of g-forces and must be proficient swimmers in case of emergency at sea. Most importantly, they are taught to fly, use their instruments, and maneuver in formations.

NAVAL FLIGHT OFFICERS

Naval Flight Officers (NFOs) are the men and women who operate the advanced systems onboard naval aircraft but do not pilot the planes. Depending on the type of plane they are assigned to, an NFO may be the Radar-Intercept Officer (RIO) who operates the complex navigation, sensor, and weapons systems onboard. NFOs may also act as the Tactical Coordinator, directing the pilot and sensor/weapons operator in attack runs on hostile submarines. A third job of NFOs is as an Electronic Countermeasures Officer (ECMO), operating the equipment that jams hostile radars and radio communications, helping to protect the plane from anti-aircraft weapons.

TOP GUN

The United States Navy Fighter Weapons School—sometimes referred to as "Top Gun" after the film of the same name—was once the most famous fighter pilot training center in the world until it merged with the Naval Strike and Air Warfare Center in Nevada.

The goal of the Naval Strike and Air Warfare Center is to train pilots in air-to-air combat tactics, as well as air-to-ground missile strikes. The United States Air Force has a similar training center called the United States Air Force Fighter Weapons School.

Instructors at the "Top Gun" academy fly the F/A-18 Hornet and the F-16 Falcon. The F-16 Falcon is used by many different countries and can therefore be used in training to simulate the threat from enemy fighter planes.

This pilot is wearing an oxygen mask to make sure he gets the air he needs when flying at extremely high altitudes.

Many fighter squadrons have nicknames like the Panthers, the Thunderbolts, the Silver Eagles, and the Ghost Riders.

Naval pilots must go through rigorous training to receive their "wings of gold."

DOGFIGHT!

THE TERM "DOGFIGHT" refers to an aerial battle between two or more fighter planes. The preferred method of attack is for a pilot to position his or her plane directly behind the enemy so that there's no danger of the enemy pilot being able to fire back. The two planes involved in the battle often have to make many passes around each other trying to get into this position. Someone once said the planes look like two dogs chasing each other's tails, and "dogfighting" came to be.

The view from the cockpit of a fighter plane is both dizzying and awe-inspiring. The plane above is in the process of making a turn.

MODERN WARFARE

Even in the jet age, modern air-to-air combat often develops into good old-fashioned dogfights. Pilots use all their skills to maximize the strengths of their planes, allowing them to move into the "kill" position.

Gaining the upper hand in a dogfight can depend on not only a pilot's experience and skill, but also the agility of his or her plane when flown at minimum air speeds. Ironically, for the new breed of supersonic jets, dogfights are generally contests fought at low airspeeds, maintaining just enough energy for sudden acrobatic maneuvering.

The pilot of this F-5 Freedom Fighter is looking over his shoulder to see the F-14 Tomcat that is sneaking up on him.

"Dogfighting" has gone to the doghouse! Modern aerial combat is now referred to as air-to-air combat and air combat maneuvering.

Modern air-to-air guided missiles, helmet-mounted sights, tail-mounted radar, and rear-firing missiles have made dogfighting a different battle than it was in the past. Pilots no longer need to gain that rear position in order to fire on the enemy. However, pilots still learn the skills of classic dogfighting, and aircraft manufacturers continue to consider dogfighting capabilities in the planes they design.

Two fighter planes usually fly together. One plane is the leader. The other is called the "wingman."

REFUELING IN MIDAIR

Stationed in the back of the refueler plane, an operator uses a control stick to maneuver the nozzle of the boom into the fuel tank of the fighter plane.

EVEN THOUGH FIGHTER JETS are designed to travel great distances on the amount of fuel they can carry in their tanks, sometimes it is necessary for the planes to refuel before they finish their mission. Instead of landing—which wastes time and may cause the plane to have to travel hundreds of miles out of the way— today's fighter jets are designed to be able to refuel on the go. A special refueling plane uses a telescoping tube called a "boom" to connect to and refuel the tank of a jet while both planes continue to fly.

WORLD WAR II

During World War II, U.S. bombers had to travel great distances from their bases in England and the Mediterranean to reach their targets in Germany. The bombers were accompanied by fighter planes whose job it was to keep the bombers safe during their mission. However, the fighter planes' small fuel tanks often forced them to turn back before the end of the mission, allowing enemy fighter planes to attack the bombers. With mid-air refueling, fighter planes were able to escort bombers through entire missions.

Modern refueling planes can hold more than 350,000 gallons of fuel and can transfer the fuel at a rate of up to 1,500 gallons per minute.

The ability to refuel in midair means a fighter plane can carry extra weapons instead of additional fuel.

PROFESSIONAL DAREDEVILS

With the wings of their planes just a few feet apart, even a tiny deviation from the course can be a major disaster for air show pilots.

I F YOU VISIT AN AIR SHOW, you can see them zipping and zooming through the air, performing acrobatic maneuvers that will make your heart race just watching. The pilots who fly in air shows perform for the public the same incredible maneuvers in the same high-tech planes that they would use in air-to-air combat missions.

During an air show, the pilots do rolls and steep dives while flying at high speeds—often while in formation with other planes. In formation, the wing tips of each plane are only three feet away from the other planes in formation. Just a tiny mistake by one pilot can mean disaster for the entire squadron.

The most famous of all stunt flying teams is the Blue Angels. The Blue Angels are a group of six pilots who travel the world performing spectacular stunts at air shows. Since their first air show back in 1946, the Blue Angels have performed for more than 414 million fans. All Blue Angel pilots are Navy or Marine Corps trained. They must have at least 1,250 flight hours in order to be selected as a Blue Angel pilot.

FIRE ENGINES

HERE COME THE TRUCKS!

You've seen them racing to the scene of a fire or emergency, sirens screaming and horns blaring. They're fire engines, rescue vehicles we depend on to keep us safe and sound. From big ladder trucks to sleek pumper trucks, fire department vehicles carry the firefighters and equipment needed to put out fires and rescue both people from burning buildings and the occasional cat stuck in a tree.

Some fire engines are a greenish-yellow color, which is easier for our eyes to see in the dark.

Although we use the terms interchangeably, a fire truck is actually different from a fire engine. Fire engines carry their own water supply, while fire trucks carry additional firefighting equipment and other emergency gear, such as rescue tools, ladders, and extrication equipment.

SP9713

Back when horses were used to pull fire equipment, Dalmations kept them company during the long waits between fires, guarding the horses and keeping them from wandering off.

IN THE HOUSE

THE FIREHOUSE IS THE HEART of the fire company. It provides overnight accommodations for firefighters on duty and comes complete with a kitchen, common rooms, and plenty of companionship.

When firefighters are not fighting a fire, they still have plenty to do at the firehouse. The crew takes turns doing the housework and cooking the meals. They also maintain their gear. From washing the fire engines to hanging the hoses to dry, they make sure that all of the equipment is ready for the next emergency.

Firefighters take turns doing the cooking and cleaning at the firehouse.

Look Out Below!

When not on call, firefighters usually spend their time on the upper levels of the firehouse where the living quarters, kitchen, and common areas can be found. The fire pole allows firefighters to get from the upper level down to the first floor—where the fire engines are located—as quickly as possible.

Firefighters always park the fire engine facing out so that they can pull out quickly on the way to a fire.

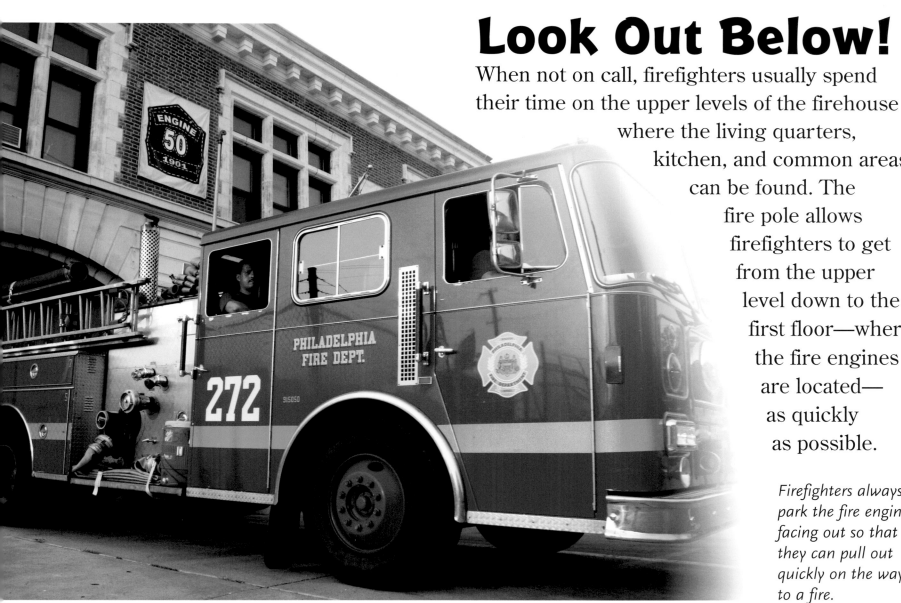

The first fire pole was installed in the house of Chicago's Engine Company No. 21 in 1878. The company was almost always the first to arrive on the scene of a fire, so eventually fire poles were installed in every firehouse in Chicago.

BECOMING A FIREFIGHTER

FIREFIGHTING CAN BE a very dangerous job. The brave men and women who risk their lives to save others know that any mistakes they make might kill or injure themselves or someone else. In the United States, the National Fire Academy is located in Emmitsburg, Maryland, and is where firefighters and other emergency workers are trained to deal more effectively with fire and related emergencies.

A student will train for 600 hours over the course of 14 weeks to become a firefighter. After leaving school, firefighters spend one year learning on the job before they can graduate. They are called "probies" because they are "on probation" until they have proven themselves over the course of the year.

Training to be a firefighter can be stressful and exhausting. Firefighters must be able to handle many different types of emergencies.

What It Takes

Being a firefighter is a difficult job, and becoming a firefighter is difficult, too. Before men and women can even begin training, they must pass a physical test. A firefighter may need to carry an injured person down several flights of stairs, or he or she may need to help carry a heavy hose close to a fire. Both of these acts require a lot of strength. After prospective firefighters show that they can handle the physical aspects of the job, they start their training, learning everything from the proper way to fold a hose to the best way to climb a ladder.

One of the most well-known fires in history is the Great Chicago Fire of 1871. Legend has it that the fire started when a cow kicked over a kerosene lantern in a barn. While this story has been proven to be false, more than one-third of the city was destroyed in the fire.

ROCKVILLE
E-32
VOLUNTEERS
"Riding With Pride"

These volunteer firefighters in Rockville, Maryland, are prepared for when the alarm sounds.

Even when a fire is out, there is still work for firefighters to do at the scene.

Fire hoses can be dangerous. The hoses shoot water with enough pressure to knock down a brick wall! Some pumper trucks can pump water at more than 2,000 gallons per minute.

How to handle a hose is just one skill firefighters need to master.

LAYING IN

WHEN HOSES ARE HOOKED UP TO A PUMPER truck or a fire hydrant and the water starts pumping, that's when the hard work really begins. Firefighters may have to carry the heavy hoses up stairs or ladders to bring the hoses as close to the fire as they can. It can take three or more firefighters to handle one hose because a hose full of water can be as heavy as a steel pipe. The hose may be so stiff that it cannot go around corners. When firefighters bring a hose close to a fire, they say they are "laying in" or "stretching in" the hose.

When they are not being used, hoses are folded or rolled up for easy access. Some fire trucks can carry hundreds or even thousands of feet of hose.

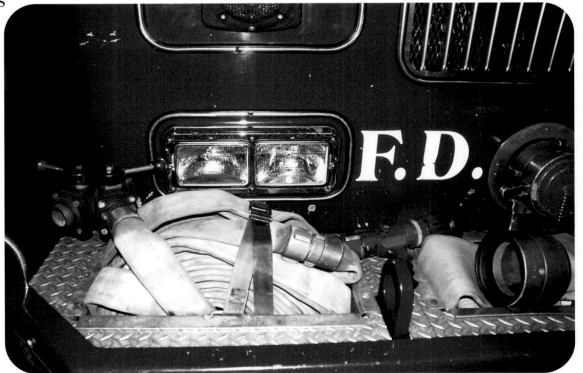

Way Back When

Before hoses were invented, people put out a fire by throwing buckets of water on it. In larger towns, neighbors would form "bucket brigades," in which the local people stood in line and passed full and empty buckets up and down between a fire and a source of water, such as a stream or a well. Not surprisingly, a lot of buildings (and even whole towns) burned to the ground with this inefficient system of firefighting.

In this photo from World War II, German civilians form a bucket brigade in an attempt to quench a fire in their village.

A fire hydrant is sometimes called a "fireplug." This is because firefighters used to make holes in the public water pipes to fight fires. After the fire was out, the holes would be plugged with stoppers. These stoppers became known as fireplugs. Fireplugs date back to at least the 1600s.

After a fire is out, firefighters use teamwork to put back all of their equipment. One of the biggest jobs is folding up the fire hose.

200 FEET

UP

DDER

OWN

OPERATOR'S STAND DOOR
MUST BE CLOSED FOR
LADDER RACK TO OPERATE

UNITED WE STAND

GOD BLESS AMERICA

Working together under dangerous conditions means that firefighters must learn to depend on each other.

MEET YOUR FIRE COMPANY

A FIRE COMPANY CONSISTS OF an officer, such as a captain or lieutenant, and several firefighters. Each company specializes in a certain task. For example, large cities may have both rescue companies—ladder or "truck" companies—and engine companies on hand to respond to different emergencies.

Fire companies often follow a "two in, two out" rule, which says that two firefighters must always enter and leave a building together. This buddy system makes sure that no one gets lost or left behind during the chaotic conditions of a fire.

Talk Like a Firefighter

Firefighters have their own words and phrases that describe what they do. Some words describe different types of fires. For example, if a firefighter says a fire is "ripe," it means that it is hot and smoky. If a fire is "a worker," it means that the firefighters will have to work very hard to put it out.

Some words firefighters use relate to what they do to put out a fire. A "fire line" (or a "fire break") is a strip of land that firefighters clear to keep forest fires from spreading. Firefighters might say they have "ventilated" a building. This means that they have opened the windows and doors, and chopped holes in the roof to let the smoke and heat out of the building.

Cutting a hole in the roof of a burning building allows smoke and heat to escape. This makes it safer for firefighters to enter the building.

When at the firehouse, firefighters take care of the engines and other equipment, but they still have time for a bit of fun.

NO. 3

2 1/2"

Pump panels feature gauges and knobs that monitor and control the water output and pressure. The panel can be located on either the side, back, or top of the truck.

PUMPER TRUCKS

PUMPER TRUCKS CARRY THE HOSES needed to fight fires and are usually the first fire engines to arrive at a fire. It is their job to get the hoses hooked up to a water source, such as a fire hydrant. Then they spray water on the building to get it cooled down enough so that firefighters can enter it. The amount and force of the water are both controlled by a pump panel. Firefighters who work on pumper trucks are sometimes called "smoke eaters" because they breathe in (or "eat up") so much smoke.

Pumper trucks can carry many feet of hose, but sometimes more hose is needed. Some fire departments have special hose trucks that carry hundreds of feet of extra hose for pumper trucks to use.

And More Pumper Trucks . . .

A rescue pumper carries specialized rescue equipment in addition to a water tank that can hold up to 500 gallons of water. Rescue pumper trucks generally carry fewer feet of hose compared to traditional pumper trucks. A super pumper truck has a water cannon that can shoot water up to 500 feet into the air. That's enough for it to go over another building and hit a target a block away!

Gauges help firefighters monitor the pressure of the water pumping through the hose. PSI stands for pounds per square inch.

WATER TANK
FILL

NO 4 REAR
3" DISCHARGE

OPEN

Waterous
DEPENDABLE

MC

PULL TO PRIME

WATER TANK
TO PUMP

IN OUT
CLOSE OPEN

OPEN

Waterous

DELUGE

IN OUT
CLOSE OPEN

OPEN

Waterous

	SEAGRAVE FIRE APR. INC. 105 E. 12TH STREET CLINTONVILLE, WI 54929	PERFORMANCE		
		G.P.M.	PRESSURE	ENGINE RPM
PRODUCTION NO.			100 PSI	
PUMP MANUFACTURE	WATEROUS		200 PSI	
PUMP SERIAL #			320 PSI	
PUMP MODEL			900 PSI	
CAPACITY		GOVERNED		RPM

RING THE BELL

IF YOU LIVE NEAR A FIREHOUSE, you may have heard the fire alarm that alerts firefighters of a fire nearby. Sometimes there may be one call of the bell. Sometimes there may be as many as five. The size of a fire is indicated by the number of bells sounded. A one-alarm fire is small and requires just one fire company to respond. A five-alarm fire is big, needing the help of multiple fire companies.

SOUND THE SIRENS

IN ORDER TO GET TO A FIRE or emergency as quickly as possible, fire engines are equipped with sirens and lights that warn people to make way and watch out for the speeding trucks. The controls for the lights and sirens are located on panels near the driver of the truck. New technology allows fire trucks to control the traffic light system, changing the lights to green as they approach, so that they can avoid accidents that are sometimes caused by fire trucks running through red lights.

The cab of a fire truck needs to be well laid-out so firefighters can see where everything is.

ACTUAL SIZE

A ladder truck is so long that it often has two drivers. The driver in the back is called a "tillerman." The tillerman's job is to steer the rear wheels of the ladder truck.

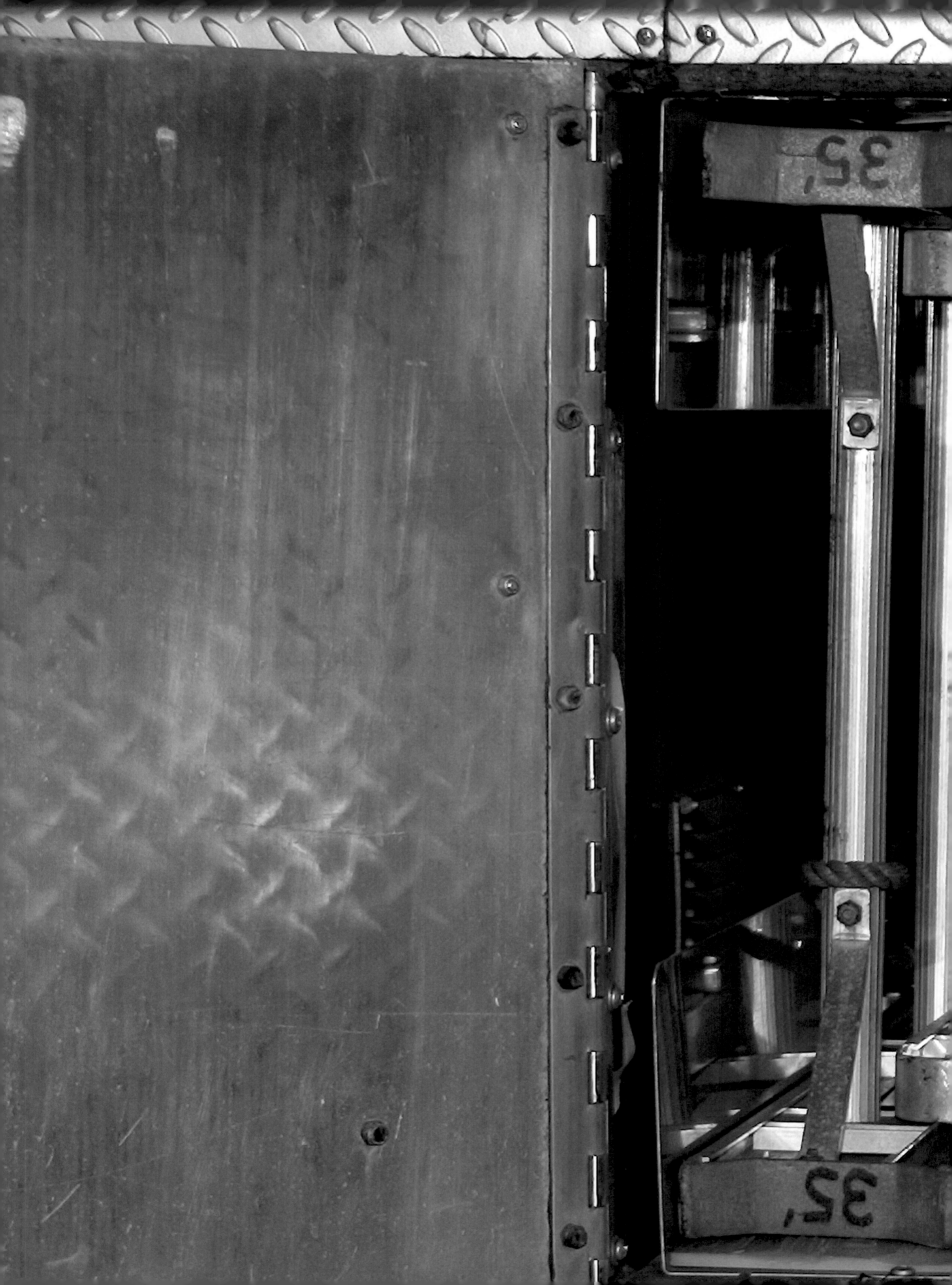

Ladder trucks have special supports called "outriggers" that hold them steady while the ladder is in use. Outriggers extend out from the sides of the fire truck, and without them, the ladder truck would be more likely to tip over.

LADDER TRUCKS

FIGHTING FIRES IN TALL BUILDINGS requires a ladder truck. Firefighters extend the ladder of the truck to get onto the high floors of high-rise buildings. They allow people trapped on the higher floors to get to the ground. The longest ladder on a fire truck is called an "aerial ladder," which can extend up to 10 floors.

Sometimes the ladder on a fire truck is the only way to get to people trapped inside a building.

Ladders on a ladder truck are as long as the truck itself—often longer!

Under Control

The control panel for an aerial ladder is located on the back of the ladder truck. The ladders are attached to turntables that allow them to turn 360 degrees. The ladder controls require just one firefighter to change the position and length of the ladder. It can take as many as six firefighters to raise a 40-foot ladder by hand, so this is a vast improvement.

Firefighters who work for a Ladder Truck Company are responsible for search and rescue, forcible entry, ventilation of a structure during a fire, and the use of ladders to rescue people above ground level.

Some ladders have a bucket at the top that provides a safe place for the firefighter to stand while the ladder is moving.

Ladder trucks also carry many freestanding ladders of different heights. These ladders can be used to get to the roofs of one-story buildings, or to second- or third-floor windows.

TOP

- 10' PIKE WOOD
- 10' PIKE WOOD
- 10' HALLIGAN W/GAS
- 10' HALL. W/GAS
- 8' ROCK
- 8' ROCK

SAFETY GEAR

FIREFIGHTERS WEAR big, metal helmets that are designed to protect a firefighter's head from both flames and falling debris. During a fire, there is always the danger of a roof caving in or other material falling down. Without proper headgear, firefighters would be risking their lives even more than they already are.

Firefighters also wear special pants, coats, and boots that are designed to keep them safe. The outfits are called "turnouts" because they are worn when firefighters "turn out" (or "show up") when there is a fire or other emergency.

Firefighters keep their suits and helmets hung up and ready to go so that they can get dressed quickly.

Fire helmets need to fit well in order to provide effective protection against flames and falling objects. Most helmets have an adjustable headband and chinstrap.

These firefighters could not enter this burning building without SCBAs.

Self-Contained Breathing Apparatus

A Self-Contained Breathing Apparatus, also known as an SCBA, helps firefighters breathe clean air while fighting smoky fires. An SCBA has three parts. The first part is a high-pressure tank carrying compressed oxygen. This is connected to a regulator that controls the flow of air. The regulator is connected to a mouthpiece or mask that goes

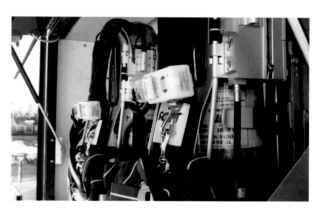

SCBAs are stored at the ready in fire trucks.

over the firefighter's face. All three parts are also attached to a harness strapped on the firefighter's back so that both hands can remain free. SCBAs are sometimes referred to as "airpacks."

Some firefighting suits are coated with metal. The metal reflects heat, keeping the firefighter from getting burned. However, the metal is heavy, which can make it difficult for firefighters to move around.

This firefighter is ready to enter a burning building.

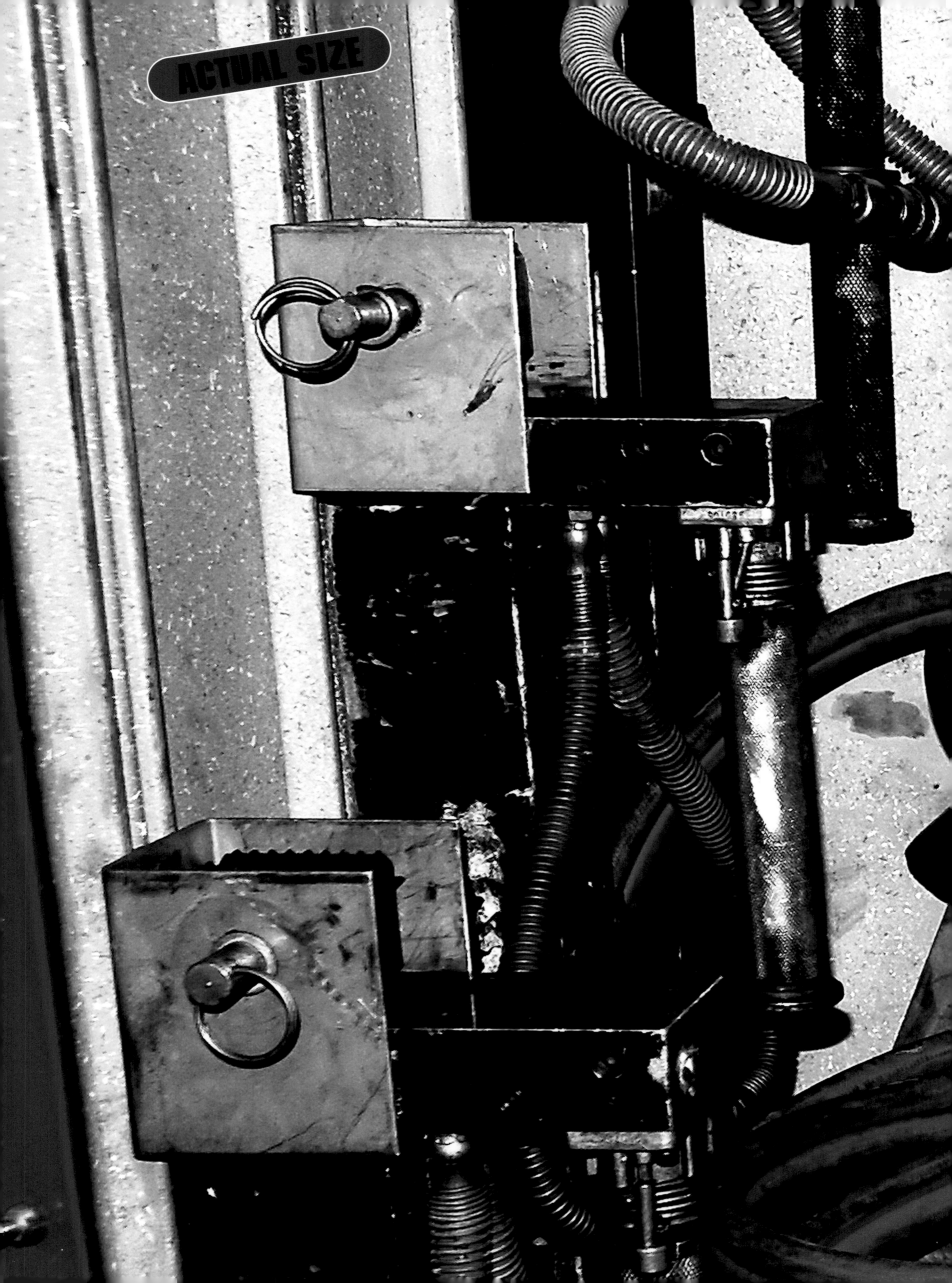

ACTUAL SIZE

FIREFIGHTING AND RESCUE EQUIPMENT

IN ADDITION TO HOSES AND LADDERS, firefighters use a variety of other equipment to save lives and extinguish fires. Some ladder trucks are called "hook and ladder trucks" because they carry hooks and other tools that can be used to tear down walls and cut through floors to get to the fire. Firefighters who use hooks are called "hookies."

A landing net is carried on the side of the fire truck, but it is used only as a last resort when a trapped person cannot or will not wait for a ladder. A landing net is only safe when used below the fourth floor of a building.

Hooks are often taller than firefighters!

High-powered nozzles help firefighters put out fires quickly.

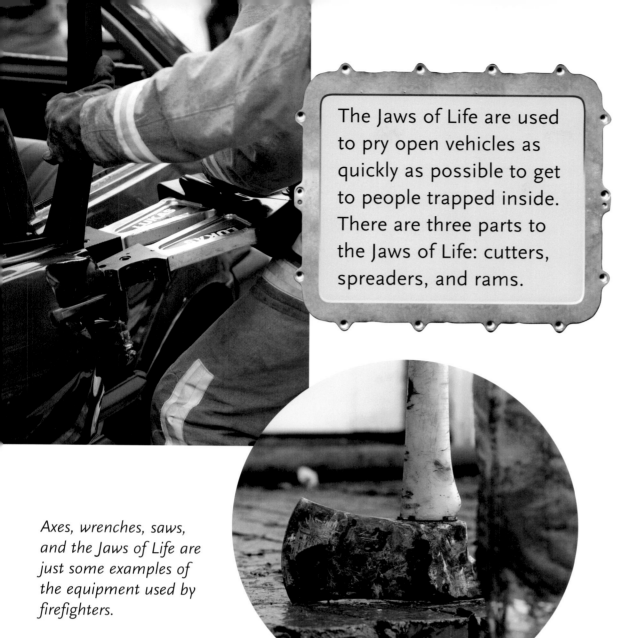

The Jaws of Life are used to pry open vehicles as quickly as possible to get to people trapped inside. There are three parts to the Jaws of Life: cutters, spreaders, and rams.

Axes, wrenches, saws, and the Jaws of Life are just some examples of the equipment used by firefighters.

This portable spotlight enables firefighters to investigate the scene after a fire has been extinguished.

There are many different kinds of nozzles that can be attached to hoses—all are stored in a special compartment on the truck.

This rescue equipment has been used to save lives in hundreds of emergencies.

THE DELUGE PUMP

THE DELUGE PUMP, ALSO KNOWN AS THE DELUGE GUN, is a special nozzle used by firefighters to spray up to 2,000 gallons of water per minute on a fire. Deluge guns are often mounted on the top of fire engines. They may also have more than one nozzle so that water can be sprayed in different directions at the same time. There is even a freestanding deluge pump that can be placed near the fire and left alone, freeing up firefighters to take on other tasks.

Deluge pumps can spray water hundreds of feet into the air.

Firefighters use fog to keep a fire contained and prevent it from spreading. Fog droplets are so small that they can stop fires without damaging clothing, furniture, artwork, and other belongings.

Beyond Water

Water doesn't work with putting out gasoline fires because the gas is able to float on top of the water and stay ignited. Gasoline fires can be put out with a foam that is made by adding chemicals to water to produce a mass of bubbles. The foam prevents air from getting to the flames. Fire needs air to keep burning, so the foam stops the fire by smothering it.

To keep a fire from spreading, this firefighter has sprayed foam on the entire area.

Deluge pumps help firefighters get the maximum amount of water where it needs to go.

FIREFIGHTING AROUND THE WORLD

THE VERY FIRST FIRE ENGINES were developed in England in the 1700s. These first engines were pulled by people, and it took 20 or more strong men to pull an engine. Once the engine reached the fire, it then had to be pumped by hand. It could take a dozen men to pump enough water to put out even a small fire. Today, fire engines in England, Canada, and across the world have the high-tech equipment designed to put a fire out as quickly as possible.

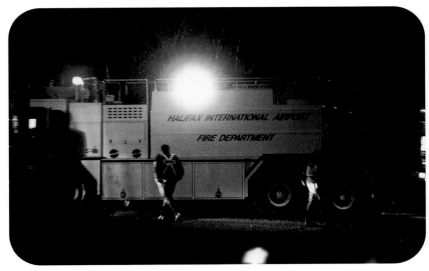

This fire engine—assigned to the Halifax, Nova Scotia, airport—is on hand in case of an accident.

French firefighters are called *sapeurs-pompiers*. They handle more than 3.6 million emergencies a year, ranging from fires to car accidents to stuck elevators.

Firefighters are extinguishing a fire after the collision of a train and a truck in northern France.

UN TRAIN PEUT E
CACHER UN AUTR

International Crews

Firefighter units in England are called "brigades." Brigades are then divided into stations that each have at least one pumper engine. The average size of a crew for a British station is five. Some countries, such as Finland, operate their fire crews with four to six firefighters. The engine carries the unit leader, an engineer, and two to four firefighters, depending on the size and intensity of the fire.

We all know that the number to call in case of emergency in the United States is 9-1-1. However, in Germany the number to call is 1-1-2. Although firefighters around the world may name things differently, most use the same type of equipment and technology to fight fires.

On November 20, 1992, Windsor Castle near London, England, caught fire. It took nearly 40 fire engines and more than 200 firefighters to put out the blaze. Luckily, no one was seriously injured in the fire.

Rescue vehicles line the streets near a train station in Bologna, Italy. In countries around the world, firefighters and other rescue personnel are always at the ready to help in whatever way they can.

HEAVY EQUIPMENT

Dump trucks use hydraulic cylinders that telescope inside each other to lift the heavy truck bed and dump the load. The telescoping cylinders allow the truck bed to be lifted high enough to dump out even the heaviest load.

THE WORLD OF HEAVY EQUIPMENT

EVERYWHERE YOU LOOK, heavy equipment is making changes to the world around us. From building skyscrapers to loading freight trains, from tearing down old houses to mining for the fuel we need, heavy equipment is used to make our world a better place.

Lots of Different Types

There are more than 25 different types of heavy equipment. There are backhoes, which dig ditches with one end and move piles of dirt with the other. There are forklifts, which move around factories and warehouses stacking cargo and loading trucks. And there are cranes, which can lift metal beams weighing thousands of pounds high into the air.

This giant dump truck is so heavy and big that it cannot travel on regular roads. It uses up to six gallons of gas for every mile it travels.

This vintage tractor resembles an army tank!

A dump truck is also called a "tipper truck" because of the way it raises its back and tips out what it is carrying.

A giant dump truck will typically be in service for 15 years. During that time, it will be in operation for around 80,000 hours.

DUMP TRUCKS

THE MOST WELL-KNOWN KIND of heavy equipment is the dump truck. There are several different kinds of dump trucks, including ones that dump their load out of the bottom of the truck instead of lifting and tilting the truck bed to pour the load out. Another kind of dump truck can dump its load to the side of the truck.

G-I-A-N-T Trucks

Imagine a dump truck bigger than a house, with tires 12 feet across and weighing four tons each. These giant dump trucks actually exist and work in mining operations all over the world. Giant dump trucks are able to carry loads of more than 200 tons, and their fuel tanks can carry 1,000 gallons of gas.

The tires on a giant dump truck each weigh the same as three cars and are taller than two people standing on each other's shoulders.

BUCKET WHEEL EXCAVATORS

SIMILAR TO THE BUCKET BRIGADES used in the early days of firefighting, the bucket wheel excavator has the ability to remove soil without stopping to dump its load. Featuring a large main wheel with buckets attached to it all around, the bucket wheel excavator works by filling the buckets with dirt, coal, or soil, and then dumping its load directly onto a conveyor belt system that takes the material away from the digging site. Bucket wheel excavators are often used for open-pit mining operations, for digging canals, and for projects that require the removal of a lot of dirt.

The largest bucket wheel excavators can remove more than three million cubic yards of material a day.

Some bucket wheel excavators are bigger than two football fields and weigh more than 29 million pounds.

Some wheels have 24 buckets—each the size of a car!

Bucket wheel excavators are most often used to dig into soft and loose materials. They aren't used very much in the United States, where the soil is typically hard and filled with large rocks.

THE SPACE SHUTTLE CRAWLER

GETTING THE SPACE SHUTTLE from its home at the Vehicle Assembly Building to the launch pad is a big job. The distance is only about four miles, but without the crawler-transporter used to move the Space Shuttle into position, it might as well be on another planet. The crawler-transporter is the largest self-powered tracked vehicle in the world. Each crawler wheel is 131 feet long, 114 feet wide, and 20 feet high.

The roadway that the crawler travels on is 130 feet wide. That's as wide as an eight-lane highway.

Moving Along

When it is not carrying a load, the crawler-transporter can move at a maximum speed of two miles per hour. When it is loaded down with the shuttle—with a combined weight of 11 million pounds—it moves approximately one mile per hour, taking more than five hours to get the Space Shuttle to the launch pad.

Standing Tall

The crawler-transporter is controlled from two cabs located at opposite ends of the machine. The operators drive the crawler-transporter along a specially made track called the crawlerway. To ensure the safety of the Space Shuttle, the crawler-transporter is designed to keep completely level at all times. Even when the Space Shuttle is raised into its launch position, it is never more than a fraction of a degree from being completely vertical.

The Vehicle Assembly Building—where the Space Shuttles are kept when they are not in use—is one of the largest buildings in the world. In fact, the inside of the building is so large that rain clouds have formed below the ceiling!

Each shoe on the crawler weighs a ton.

Draglines sit above the area that is being excavated and dump the material from a new hole into the last hole that was dug or into waiting dump trucks.

MARVELOUS MINING MACHINES

DRAGLINES ARE MACHINES that use large metal buckets to dig deep into the earth to uncover the minerals hidden below. The largest draglines use as many as 40 motors to generate the power needed to work 24 hours a day, seven days a week, without stopping. It takes two people to operate these machines.

The buckets on a dragline can be as large as 220 cubic yards, but they are typically much smaller, in the 10- to 150-cubic-yard range. The bucket on a dragline is attached to a boom that extends over the material that is being removed. The boom can be as long as a football field.

A 150-cubic-yard bucket can loosen, scoop, and move more than 200 tons of dirt in only 90 seconds.

The world's growing demand for energy is creating a need for more giant draglines, which are often the easiest and most cost-effective way to reach the minerals and resources that are underground.

The Biggest of the Big

Weighing up to 28 million pounds and standing more than 22 stories high, giant mining machines are rarely used these days. Mining operators have discovered that these huge machines—with names like "The Captain" and "Big Brutus"—are not cost-effective to operate because of the high fuel and maintenance costs.

Overburden

Overburden is the term used to describe the dirt and debris that cover up whatever is being mined. It is often the job of mining equipment to break up the overburden and then remove it from the mine, allowing the coal, phosphate, or other mineral deposits to be collected.

Each dragline is designed to work in a particular mine. It can take three years to design and build a dragline, which can last 30 to 40 years with proper maintenance.

A dragline can remove larger amounts of soil cheaper than a shovel-and-truck combination.

The basic concept of draglines has not changed much since the original design was developed in 1904.

Eleven tunnel-boring machines—each weighing 450 tons—were used to build the Channel Tunnel linking England to the European mainland.

The first machine that would attempt to create a tunnel under the English Channel between England and France was built in the 1870s.

A "BORING" MACHINE

• •

A TUNNEL-BORING MACHINE is basically a gigantic drill. It works by cutting into rock with a force of more than 10 million pounds. In the front of the machine is a cutter that rotates slowly, usually not more than eight times per minute. As the cutter moves, it removes the rock, which is then taken away on a conveyor belt.

The cutting head of a full-face tunnel-boring machine can be anywhere from 6 to 36 feet in diameter, and have three to eight radial arms.

The Channel Tunnel

Building the Chunnel—the longest tunnel in the world—between England and France took 11 tunnel-boring machines more than 99 months. The cutters on the boring machines were as big as 26 feet wide and turned at a rate of 3.3 rotations per minute with a force of up to 4,220 tons. That's a lot of force!

A "cutterhead" has a series of rotating discs operated by chains fitted with picks mounted at the end of a boom.

The force for the cutting edge of a full-face tunnel-boring machine is provided by hydraulic rams.

ACTUAL SIZE

A log loader, like the one seen here, is similar to an excavator. The basic machines are the same, but they have different attachments.

TIMBER!

TO GET THE WOOD WE NEED for construction—as well as the ingredients for paper and more than 5,000 other products—trees are cut down using heavy equipment: tree harvesters. A 15-ton tree harvester is similar to a small excavator. Like the excavator, it has a boom that can reach about 30 feet. The boom carries a harvesting head that has saws, grips, and debarkers.

To cut a tree, the machine operator first programs the machine to cut the tree to a certain length. Next, the grips are attached to the base of the tree, and the saw cuts the tree from the bottom. The machine then pulls the tree through the harvesting head so that the debarker can remove the bark and tree limbs.

A tree harvester operated by one person takes less than 30 seconds to cut, delimb, and debark a 100-foot-tall tree.

At the preprogrammed length, the tree is cut again and the log falls to the ground. Then the machine repeats the process until the entire tree is cut into identical-length logs.

Today's forestry equipment is designed to cut down and remove trees without harming anything else in the forest.

This Up Close photo shows the gears
on a tracked vehicle like the ones
used in forestry and construction.

DRILLING FOR BLACK GOLD

DRILLING FOR OIL requires some of the largest, most complicated equipment ever created. Capable of drilling more than five miles into the ground to find "black gold," oil rigs can be found both on land and offshore. Offshore oil rigs stand more than 1,000 feet tall and can support a crew of more than 300 people for months at a time.

Today's high-tech oil rigs can pump as much as 250,000 barrels of oil every day.

An offshore oil rig is built on hollow concrete supports called caissons. Caissons are built on shore and then towed by a tugboat to where the rig will be built.

Sitting on caissons high above the water, this oil-drilling platform must be able to withstand severe weather conditions such as hurricanes.

Today's modern tractors have air conditioning, a space for a laptop computer, adjustable armrests, and even cup holders.

TERRIFIC TRACTORS

GIANT TRACTORS WORK HARD to help America's farmers harvest crops and cultivate the land. With as many as 12 six-foot-high-tires, more than 400 horsepower, and a computerized control panel that tells the operator how many acres have been plowed, today's tractors are examples of modern machinery at its finest.

It used to take dozens of people and animals to plow a field. Today, one high-tech tractor can do the same work in less time.

Today's tractors have advanced hydraulic systems.

There are many different kinds of tractor attachments. *Plows* prepare the field for the planting of crops; *cultivators* break up the soil to allow air and water to reach all the plants; and *haymakers* and *balers* help the farmer harvest the crops.

As large as they are, the wheels on a tractor are designed to move among crops without damaging them.

This old tractor plowed hundreds and hundreds of acres in its day.

The Harvest Brigade

The combine harvester, also known as the combine, is one machine that is able to do all the elements of farming in a single step. For example, it can cut the grain, remove the seeds, and spit out the straw and chaff at a rate of 100 acres per day.

Because different crops require slightly different harvesting mechanisms, combines are fitted with removable attachments that are each designed for a particular crop. These attachments are called headers.

Working together, these two combines can harvest dozens of acres per day.

PAVING THE WAY

EVERY MILE YOU DRIVE, the wheels of your car smoothly rolling over the surface of the road, is thanks to the work of a paving machine. In the years since the beginning of the construction of the national highway system in the 1950s and 1960s, pavers have become an essential part of the heavy equipment arsenal.

Pavers are designed to perform two different tasks. First, they lay down the asphalt or concrete that is going to be paved onto a specially prepared surface. Then, they shape the material to the correct form, which is usually a flat surface. Modern paving machines can move at a pace of about 20 feet per minute.

Asphalt pavers have two parts. The first is the tractor that powers the machine. The second part distributes and shapes the material.

Asphalt is made from crushed stone, sand, gravel, and other materials mixed with tar.

Flatter than a Pancake

The runways at major airports must have a thickness of 20 to 25 inches, and be perfectly flat and completely level to accommodate the incredible weight of an airplane during both takeoff and landing. Because the expected lifespan of a runway is only 20 years—with a cost of as much as $90 million and thousands of tons of concrete needed—creating a new runway is an important and costly undertaking.

The smallest pavers are hand-held machines. The largest pavers can be as big as 150 feet across.

Asphalt requires heat to be molded into a flat surface. Vibrations are used to get rid of any bubbles that form.

Mining bulldozers may be operated up to 2,700 hours a year—more than twice as much as a construction company bulldozer would work in the same amount of time.

SUPER DOZERS

A BULLDOZER IS ONE of the simplest ideas in heavy machinery. Designed only to push dirt or other material out of the way, bulldozers can be found everywhere from construction sites to battlefields. Bulldozers use wheels or crawlers to move steadily over almost any terrain.

Bulldozer Blades

The blades on a bulldozer can be different, depending on their intended purpose. There are three basic types of blades. An "S," or straight, blade is used for fine grading, making an area level by moving the dirt out of the way. A "U," or universal, blade has large side wings, making it able to move more material than an "S" blade. A combination of these two blades, called an "S-U," is used for pushing even larger piles of materials.

This bulldozer blade has spikes that help it scoop up rocks and other hard debris.

Bulldozers also have a rear attachment called a ripper. The ripper is used to remove stumps, rocks, or anything else that can't easily be moved out of the way.

ACTUAL SIZE

This bulldozer crawler can climb piles of dirt, over fallen trees, and can easily get where it needs to go.

The Biggest Bulldozer

Bulldozers come in many different sizes, from small (less than 100 horsepower) to large (770 horsepower) to extra large (more than 1,000 horsepower). The biggest bulldozer ever built weighed 300,000 pounds and was powered by a 1,150-horsepower engine. With a blade almost 11 feet high and 25 feet wide, and the machine itself more than 38 feet long, the Komatsu D575A-2 was as big as a two-bedroom house!

This average-size bulldozer uses hydraulics to lift incredible amounts of weight.

The term "bulldozer" was used before modern bulldozers were invented. First used in 1876, to "bull doze" meant to bully or intimidate someone. It wasn't until the 1930s that modern machines were called bulldozers.

The bolts on a bulldozer must withstand a lot of wear and tear—and the elements.

ACTUAL SIZE

ACTUAL SIZE

Some bulldozers are steered with a control stick.

Engine rpm and travel
controlled by a warn
during cold starts.
Manual.

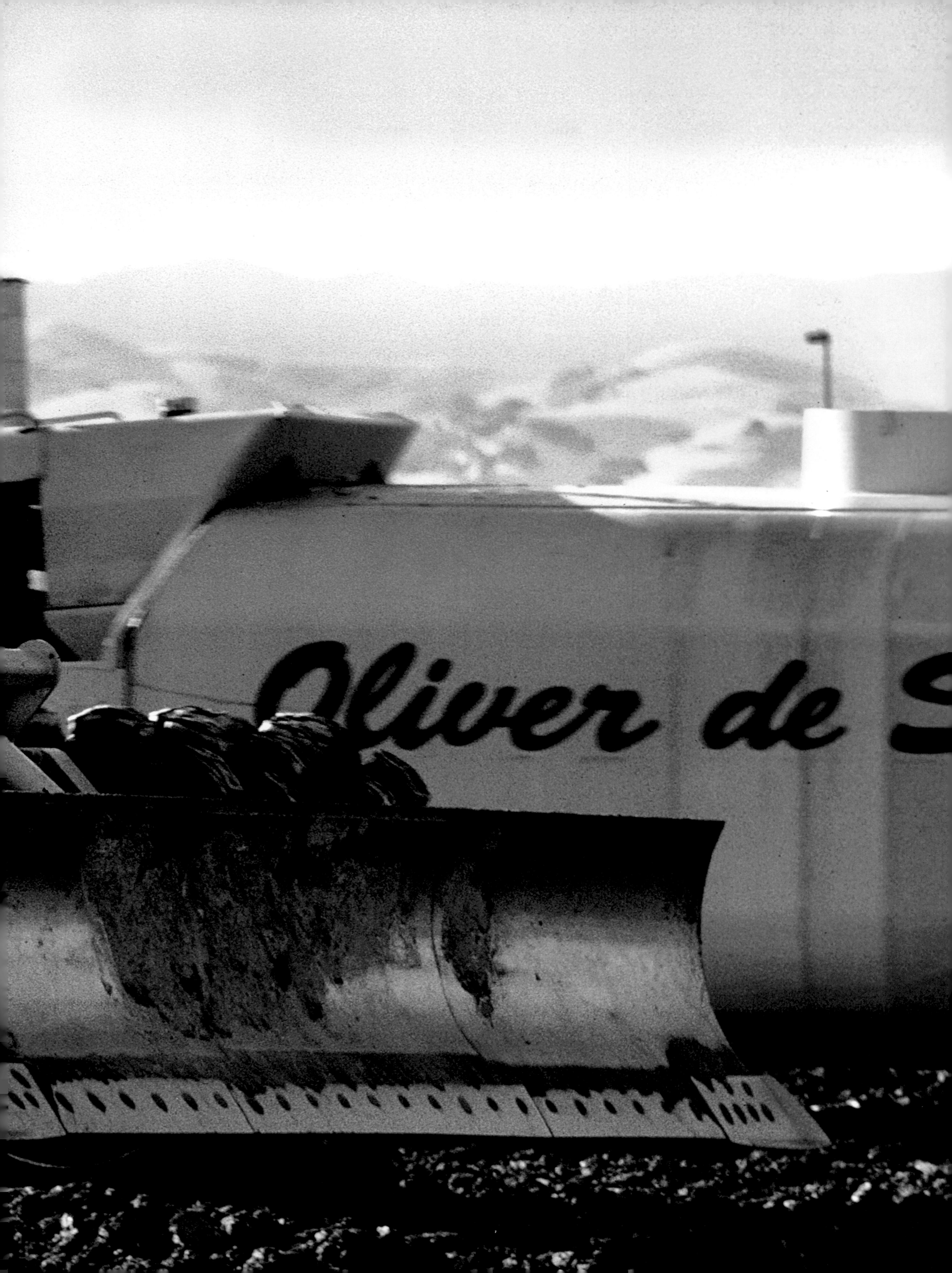
Oliver de

REDUCE, REUSE, RECYCLE

ACTUAL SIZE

EVERY WEEK, MILLIONS OF AMERICANS put their recyclable waste out to be collected. Have you ever wondered what happens to all those cans and bottles? Well, they are taken to places with recycling equipment that sorts the materials, smashes them into reusable bits, and then changes them into a new form. There are many different types of recycling equipment for wood, metal, and plastics. In the shredder category alone, there are bottle shredders, tire shredders, paper shredders, and more. There are also chippers, granulators, pulverizers, shearers, and crushers!

Some recycling equipment crushes recyclables into bales like those seen below.

The grabber on this machine picks up materials and deposits them somewhere else.

Recycling Breakthrough

Alton Newell, a junkyard manager, was looking for a more efficient way to recycle the metal found in cars and other pieces of machinery. In the 1960s, he created a machine that has a rotor with steel discs and hammers that cut the metal into pieces as small as 3 x 4 inches. This machine, called the Newell Shredder, can reduce a car to scrap metal in about 30 seconds.

A baling press can take a bulky metal object, such as a car, and compress it from all sides until it resembles a giant metal block.

Compactors

In a compactor, everything from tin cans to cars can be compressed into a smaller space. The most common use of a compactor is in a garbage truck. Compressing the garbage in the back of the truck reduces the number of times the truck has to empty its load.

AMAZING CRANES

You see them towering over half-built skyscrapers—cranes, which are mobile lifting machines capable of hoisting more than 1,000 pounds hundreds of feet into the air. Today's cranes come in many forms, including truck-mounted, tower, and crawler.

Crawler Cranes

Crawler cranes have the ability to work in rocky, uneven, or shifting terrain. A common place to see crawler cranes is at a port, where they are often used to quickly load and unload ships, barges, and docks. Other crawler cranes work together with tower cranes mounted on top of buildings under construction.

The long boom on a crane must be designed to apply a counterweight to whatever the crane is lifting. Otherwise, the crane would tip over when lifting heavy loads. However, engineers must be careful that the counterweight doesn't cause the crane to tip over backward when it is not carrying a heavy load.

A tower crane has the advantage of taking up little surface area on the ground and may have a greater lifting capacity than a mobile crane.

The long, wide tracks of a crawler crane spread the weight of the vehicle over a large surface, giving the machine traction and stability.

This cable drum controls the length of 12 cables on a crawler crane.

Index

Photo Credits